When
Going to Pieces
Holds You
Together

Other books by William A. Miller:

Why Do Christians Break Down?
Big Kids' Mother Goose

When Going to Pieces Holds You Together

WILLIAM A. MILLER

AUGSBURG PUBLISHING HOUSE
Minneapolis, Minnesota

WHEN GOING TO PIECES HOLDS YOU TOGETHER

Copyright © 1976 Augsburg Publishing House

Library of Congress Catalog Card No. 76-3853

International Standard Book No. 0-8066-1543-5

All rights reserved. No part of this book may be used or reproduced in any manner whatsoever without written permission except in the case of brief quotations embodied in critical articles and reviews. For information address Augsburg Publishing House, 426 South Fifth Street, Minneapolis, Minnesota 55415.

Scripture quotations unless otherwise noted are from the Revised Standard Version of the Bible, copyright 1946, 1952, and 1971 by the Division of Christian Education of the National Council of Churches.

MANUFACTURED IN THE UNITED STATES OF AMERICA

Contents

To
The Memory of
My Father and Mother
and son, Karl Andrew

Preface

Grief is an integral part of the process and experience of life. No human being exists who is immune to loss and the resultant dynamics of grief. As a matter of fact, to a lesser or greater degree, loss and grief are virtually an everyday occurrence for most of us. However, because we tend to be so caught up in the busyness of life, few of us recognize these daily, more or less minor losses and their accompanying feelings of grief, and we focus only on those major experiences which demand the attention of all concerned.

For instance, there is a strong tendency for us to associate grief only with the loss of a loved one through death. This is unfortunate, because to varying degrees, the dynamics of grief are present in the experience of virtually *any* loss, whether it be great or small. It seems that the intensity of the experience of grief and the duration of the time needed to work it through are directly related to the personal value of the lost loved object and how much the griever cared about it.

Nevertheless, even though grief over loss by amputation, or surgery, or marital separation, or children leaving home, or by overcoming chemical dependency, manifests many of the same dynamics, grief over the loss of a loved one by death still remains the primary focus of attention, probably because *this* experience of grief is usually the most traumatic, the most intense and the longest-lasting of all.

Interestingly enough, though the whole subject of death and dying has finally been brought out of the closet, the focus of this movement has quite consistently been on the person of the one who is dying and on the subject of death itself; and comparatively little has been done with understanding the dynamics of grief and anticipatory grief experienced by the mourner.

During the past decade many of the taboos surrounding the subject of death have disappeared. In fact, that old, virtually indiscussible subject has become one of the most widely discussed matters on the American scene. We have been exposed to books, pamphlets, lectures, seminars, retreats, study groups and research projects. There has in fact, grown up an organized study of death known as thanatology. In this process a tremendous amount of valuable insight has been brought to the surface. People are looking at death in the light rather than in the dark. Attitudes are changing, and I believe, becoming more realistic, helpful and constructive.

In the midst of the expanding interest in dealing with death, I began, some years ago, to provide seminars on the subject for nursing personnel in the hospital where I am employed as chaplain. Initially this was simply an opportunity for nursing personnel to explore their personal attitudes and feelings about death, and to deal with the dying process in terms of how to relate to people who were dying.

Before long however, it became evident that another dimension needed to be considered because of its ever-presence in death situations: namely the matter of understanding and relating to the grieving relatives and friends when a patient dies.

Understandably those of us who are involved in the so-called helping professions want to help people. We want to make the sick, well; the disintegrated, whole; the sad, happy. In these groups of nursing personnel there appeared to be a genuine desire to help mourners, but some lack of clarity in understanding the manifestations of grief and the behaviors of the grievers, and therefore some question as to *how* to help them in an appropriate and therapeutic way. It was evident that sometimes because of lack of understanding or because of fear, a person would move in to discourage a certain behavior in a griever when in fact that particular behavior was a therapeutic aspect of the grief process. And thus instead of helping the griever, such well-meant "intervention" hindered and impeded the process of grief work.

The result was that in the seminars we began to talk about understanding the dynamics of grief, learning to identify behaviors in grievers which are truly integrative and health-producing *even though on the surface or at first glance they may appear to be inappropriate.*

Out of those seminars and presentations has come this book. It is based largely upon my experience and observations as a parish pastor and a clinical chaplain in a medical center. It incorporates, in addition, the experience and observations of scores of colleagues who have also dealt intensely with people in grief and mourning and who have shared with me their wisdom and insight. I am particularly grateful to Chaplain Kenneth G. Reiners of Minneapolis, for his permission to incorporate his *Diary of a Family Encounter with Grief* which he wrote in memory of his father-in-law, Mr. William C. Falk.

Because grief is universal and no one escapes its universality, this book is for all persons. If at the moment you are experiencing grief yourself, it will help you understand yourself better. It will help you also to be aware of what is happening to and in others who are grieving so that you will be better able to give them understanding, acceptance, comfort and support. You will be better able to help the griever utilize his/her own resources.

Because grief over loss is so closely related to religious experience, the book is of particular interest to persons with religious orientation. Sometimes in acting out the dynamics of their grief, grievers may appear to behave contrary to traditionally held religious principles; their words and actions may seem foreign to religious "propriety." Much more often than not however, the natural expressions of grief are well supported and even encouraged by orthodox Christian theology, and the book endeavors to make this clear.

It will become evident rather quickly that this book is not so much an analysis of the process of grief work as it is an examination of some of the natural reactions, behaviors, and expressions which people in grief manifest. It deals only with the emotional manifestations of grief, not the somatic. It is a look at how people who are experiencing grief think, talk, act and express their feelings, and an examination of how helpful these behaviors are in terms of effective grief work. The purpose of the book is to help the reader to be aware of and understand some of the more significant dynamics of the grieving process, and in that awareness and understanding to realize the truth of the title of the book. For it *is* true that in the midst of the experience of grief and mourning, what the casual observer often defines as "going to pieces" will be the very experience that will "hold you together."

1

Loss

An introduction to grief

It is a terrible experience—sometimes even terrify-
ing—to lose something of real value. The feelings that
run through us when we realize that we have suffered
a loss are legion. We think things, we say things, we
do things that seem to be totally alien to the way we
were before the loss. And even though we seem intuitively to know in our grief that this is all natural,
the loss continues to generate all kinds of "stuff" within and without, and we are frightened.

Anxiety has a field day! "What on earth am I going to do?" There is helplessness, despair, loneliness.
"I can't think. I can't think straight. My God, I must
be losing my mind!" There is a feeling of weariness,
fatigue. "I have been betrayed; this should not be happening to me." There is vascillation between acceptance
and denial. Not to mention guilt, fear, anger, self-pity.
Grief is a complex syndrome of feelings.

People generally behave strangely in the midst of

loss. They sometimes come unglued. They "fall apart." Lucille Morgan cried hysterically when her husband died. He had recently retired, and the two of them had just started out on a long-planned and eagerly anticipated vacation trip. In the airport her husband suffered a heart attack, and died not long after being brought to the hospital. In a ritualistic fashion Lucille sobbed over and over, "Oh, if only we had gotten him to the hospital sooner. If only we hadn't started out on that trip. If only I hadn't argued with him."

On the other hand, Bob Hancock didn't cry at all when his wife died. He mapped out a triangular path in the hospital lounge and paced it like a caged tiger. Occasionally he would pause in his pacing and heave a deep sigh, stare at the floor, and then take up again where he had left off.

When Martin Johnson's father died, Martin was furious. He shouted and swore at the nurses, condemned the hospital, almost struck a doctor and told the chaplain that he could very well do without "that kind of God" who would take his father from him.

People *do* strange things when they are thrown into the experience of a loss. At least many people who observe them consider them strange, and even frightening. Such a loss as death and many "lesser" losses produce the experience of grief, and grief can indeed generate what seem to be strange and frightening behaviors.

I choose to call grief an experience rather than an

emotion because it is such a complex of emotions, feelings, spiritual states, behaviors and thought processes that I doubt that anyone can adequately consider it as any one thing. It is associated almost exclusively with loss, but should not be limited to only the loss created by death.

Unfortunately we rarely think of grief outside of the death experience. And in so doing we fail to recognize that many of the dynamics of grief may be present in and experienced by the person *who loses anything of real value which he or she cares about.*

For example, grief may be experienced as the result of severe incapacitation of a loved one or of oneself—loss of the use of one's body because of paralysis, illness or accident. Severe physical or emotional disability can generate grief. It is also commonly experienced as a result of loss of part of one's physical self—internal organs by surgery, or limbs or body parts by amputation. Learning you or a loved one has an incurable disease can produce grief. The loss of something to which one has become addicted or highly dependent can produce grief—giving up smoking, or giving up alcohol or the use of drugs; even giving up certain foods because of a restricted diet. A romantic breakup can produce grief, especially if one feels jilted. A common source of grief is marital separation. Losing one's spouse through divorce can produce many symptoms of deep grief. Losing one's job, or losing a cherished position, say in school or club, can bring grief to a person. Having to pull up roots and leave home, or moving one's home to a new community can generate grief. So can the loss of children leaving home for college or military service or marriage. And retirement, too, can bring real feelings of grief.

This listing is by no means meant to be considered as an exhaustive inclusion of all the possible grief-producing experiences of life. Rather it is intended to indicate that there are indeed a great many sources of the grief experience; and in fact *the loss of anything of real value which a person cares about can produce grief.*

These seem to be important factors in understanding grief. Not only have I lost some*thing,* but it is something of value, something which has provided me with security or support or satisfaction and fulfillment, something in which I have been invested emotionally, something which I truly care about. Most of the time the loss needs to be considered more subjectively than objectively, and I need to be less aware of *what* I actually lost and more aware of what I *believe* I lost (how important it was to me). For instance, if I am laid off from my job do I simply describe this as a disappointment because I now have no source of income and must find a new source? Or do I perceive my loss of job as a very real threat to my self-worth? In other words am I grieving more the loss of my job or the loss of my feeling of self-worth—the loss of a high and positive opinion of myself? If it is the latter, my experience of grief will probably be much more extensive and intensive than if it is the former; and the former alone is bad enough.

It is not unusual for grievers to be unaware of the deeper significance of their loss, but to *feel,* nevertheless, the deeper agony, and then to wonder why they are experiencing an intensity of grief which seems to them to be excessive. Grievers say to themselves, "I shouldn't be *this* upset over my loss." But the fact is that there is often more at stake in a loss than meets the eye.

There seems to be a positive correlation between the value of the lost loved object and the intensity and duration of the grief experience. In other words, the more important and valuable to me the lost loved object was—the more I truly cared about it—the greater will be the magnitude of my mourning and the longer it will take me to work through the grief process. The more of myself I have invested emotionally in what is now lost, the more I will feel threatened. The converse of this is of course true also.

The true value of the lost loved object to the griever is however, not always general public knowledge. In human relationships for instance, it is not safe to assume that the closest relatives of the deceased will be the deepest mourners. Sometimes by virtue of circumstance a friend may mourn the loss of a person more than that person's spouse or children. This is particularly true in a family where interactions and relationships are tolerated only for the sake of appearance—where the family stays together merely to keep up the front. If a member of that family dies, there will probably be relatively little true grief within the other members of the family because they did not have that much of their emotional selves invested in the one who has died—their loss is not so threatening. However, a friend—a colleague, a work associate, a neighbor—may feel deeply grieved at this person's death because in *their* relationship, much of the self had been invested, the relationship was one of mutual support, and the friend sincerely *cared* about the deceased. The loss experienced by the friend is substantial; the loss was threatening, and the friend feels the great weight of grief. An uninformed person casually observing the mourners' display of grief at this person's death may wonder why this friend of the deceased is going to pieces so when the family is holding up so well. (This of course assumes that all the mourners are expressing their grief feelings authentically which, unfortunately is not always the case.)

Though it is important to realize the broad inclusiveness of grief—that the dynamics of grief may be present whenever we lose anything of real value which we truly care about—we can probably best understand the dynamics of grief *in general* by looking specifically at the results experienced by the loss of death.

Therefore in the chapters that follow, as we consider individually the components making up the syndrome of grief, I will focus on them as they appear in the experience of grief as a result of the loss of a loved one through death.

2

Keep Calm

The pressure to suppress

Grief is an experience which generally seems to carry with it great depth and intensity of feeling. Phrases in definitions of grief speak of "acute sorrow," "intense emotional suffering," "deep sadness," "severe emotional pain." Words like "anguish," "injury," "lament," "estrangement," "separation," "hurt" appear consistently. A great and complex syndrome of feelings wells up in the griever and calls out for some kind of expression. But because the magnitude and the diversity of this collection of feelings is often so great, those who grieve become frightened and feel reluctant to admit its presence even to themselves. To admit these feelings to others is even more difficult. And to allow them authentic expression may be next to intolerable.

The reasons for people's reluctance to express their feelings of the grief experience are many and varied, both internal and external to the griever. Generally, the reasons seem to focus around the concept of control. Usually control appears as a highly valued aspect of human personality. Particularly here in America the development of control in the developing personality is highly regarded and seen as a very positive sign of growth towards maturity. Being able to control oneself and behave rationally is considered to be a significant indicator of maturity. In our society it is rewarded and positively reinforced whenever it is manifested.

On the other hand, its opposite—being out of control and behaving irrationally—is regarded as a very negative thing in American culture and society. People who are out of control are actually socially unacceptable. They may be tolerated, but even then it is with disdain. At worst they are fined or hospitalized or imprisoned. Generally speaking, uncontrolled behavior is acceptable only in the form of group or mob action at a sports event. I think most of us are familiar with the many irrational behaviors which are manifested in the sports arena by people who are otherwise rational and very much in control of themselves. There, one is allowed almost literally to get away with murder. (For instance, "Kill the umpire!" "Murder the bum!") There, expressions of feeling which are sometimes completely uncontrolled and irrational are accepted.

One important thing to note is that people who are out of control are unpredictable and therefore frightening. It is very difficult to predict how a person who is out of control is going to act next, or how he or she is going to respond or react to a situation. People who are in control are much more predictable and safe. Furthermore, people who are in control of themselves are rational, and it is possible to get them to make sense. In all, being out of control makes for a frightening atmosphere and a potential for disorder and even chaos. On the other hand, being in control makes for good order, safety and security.

I do not wish to place value judgments on either of these opposites. Nor do I wish to sound as though I am advocating either "no controls" or "super control." All I wish to do is to stress how strongly we seem to emphasize and reward being in control, and how even more strongly we *reject* being out of control. As far as I am concerned personally, a unification of these opposites is the most desirable position, recognizing both the positive and negative aspects of each side. But even that seems to many to be too threatening to allow.

Perhaps the concept of control is not the appropriate thing here in my consideration of people's reluctance to admit to and express the variety of feelings which make up the syndrome of grief. But, I don't think so. What is it but being out of control when grieving people cry and sob and wail and moan; or verbalize hot anger addressing it to a dead person, or to God, or to an innocent bystander; or make no sense in their idealizations and rationalizations; or pace the floor, ritualistically sitting down and standing up; or lament their behavior which was actually commendable and heap great loads of inappropriate guilt upon themselves? Many indeed are the people who are quick to identify the griever as a person who is out of control and who should "get it together" and get in control.

We may not fine or hospitalize or imprison grievers who are out of control; but we certainly do sedate them, convert them, divert them and do our utmost to *get them to stop being so threatening.*

My observation is that there exists within us human beings a natural tendency to express feelings. Plain and simply, the Creator has made us that way. In fact I believe it is so much a part of our natural being that we oftentimes have to work diligently *not* to let our feelings out. We have to go out of our way to prevent the feelings from expressing themselves. We must suppress them, or we unconsciously repress them.

Now it is indeed true that if we only acted on raw feelings and gave free rein to them, our being out of control would lead only to disorder and chaos. There is no question but what we need the reins of good manners, politeness, respect for others and self, and propriety. But what is most desirable is to unify these opposites of suppression of feelings on the one hand and impulsive expression on the other; the goal is never the obliteration of either one for the other. And if the expression of authentic feelings, or appearing to be out of control, is appropriate anywhere, it is on the part of the grievers and in the expression of their grief —frightening though it may be.

The inner inhibitor within the griever is, I believe, the result of external sources. Without the external sources I believe a griever's inner voice would allow him or her to express the authentic feelings of grief without fear of rejection or reprisal. However as it is, the griever's inner voice often sounds like this: "If I let my feelings find expression, what will people say of me? Or worse yet, what will they *think* of me and never say, except behind my back? People are always observing and evaluating. What is *expected* of me? What am I *supposed* to do? How *should* I behave in this? I want people's respect. I want their commendation."

A young woman who was caught up in grief over the condition of her little child appeared physically to be quite distraught. Nevertheless she smiled benevolently and spoke softly. As we talked together about what was going on inside her in the midst of this grief she said to me smilingly, "I don't know how I am supposed to act in a situation like this." She wanted to go to pieces, but she rather doubted that that was the acceptable behavior for her situation.

There is indeed this inner inhibitor which works against a natural and healthy expression of authentic feelings in the time of grief. Most of us in America have learned the accepted and official rules of the game of grief-expression early in life. And we have been appropriately rewarded for obeying and punished for disobeying. So that for most of us the conditioning has been quite effective and we have learned well.

I believe that most of the time personal protection and survival is the primary motive at work when people discourage or inhibit others in their expression of grief feelings. I mean, if it is true that grieving people expressing their feelings openly and authentically appears to me to be out of control and I am frightened by that, I will do whatever I can to encourage them not to behave in that manner. It will make a lot of sense to me to do what I can to prevent it, if I see a person going to pieces right before my eyes. Self-preservation is clearly evident here. More often than not I will encourage grievers not to behave the way they are behaving *not* because I really believe it would be more helpful, more therapeutic or more integrating for them not to behave that way, but because that behavior frightens me, I don't know what to expect next and I don't think I can handle it. So I say to them, "Please help *me* by changing *your* behavior and suppressing *your* feelings."

Of course that is not at all what I say to the griever. What I *actually* say are things like: "Can I get you a mild sedative to help you relax?" "Don't fret. You'll be OK. Time heals all things." "Chin up; you *have* faith, don't you?" "Oh well, think of all the wonderful memories you have." "You know she is much better off." "Just get yourself busy and find new interests." "There now, big boys don't cry."

There is an actual collusion that goes on here. The inner voice of inhibition in the griever and the external pressure of "society" to be stoic join and form a conspiracy against the nature of the griever which is to express authentically the real feelings of the grief experience. And the conspiracy succeeds every time the griever obeys and "pulls herself together." Successfully suppressing the various feelings of grief may win the support of society ("My, didn't she hold up well!"), but the price of the pain of loss must be paid at some time. The human psyche will exact payment with interest.

As we shall see in the chapters that follow many of the behaviors performed by grieving people do indeed appear to be strange and frightening. By some of our society's standards the griever may definitely appear to be going to pieces. But the point is that even though this may be true, in order to retain wholeness and spiritual and emotional health in the experience of loss, it is necessary to express the feelings and work through the dynamics of grief. Being stoic—brave, tough, bearing up—may be admired by society as real strength and rewarded as a virtue, but it is nothing less than conscious suppression or unconscious repression or denial, and an avoidance of grief work.

As we look at the various dynamics of grief it will become clear that the phrase "grief work" is indeed appropriate. Grief work is called grief work because that is precisely what it is—work. Grief needs to be worked through, worked out, worked off. And it *will be* somehow, somewhere, sometime; either constructively or destructively, partially or completely, in an integrating fashion or disintegrating, health restoring or health destroying, as good grief or bad grief, at the time of the loss or years removed. There is little point in dwelling on what *may* happen to a person if grief over a loss is not expressed and worked through. What is true of the suppression, repression or denial of *any* feeling is certainly true of the feelings making up the grief syndrome.

Surely everyone knows of someone who "successfully" passed through a grief experience without shedding a tear, holding up magnificently, immediately finding new interests and keeping busy with friends and new acquaintances, only to begin to lose touch with reality a few months after the loss and to be admitted to a hospital for treatment of an emotional breakdown.

Sylvia Plath in her thinly disguised autobiography, *The Bell Jar,* clearly demonstrates the frightening power of repressed grief. She tells how on a visit to her father's grave she was seized with overwhelming grief. At the grave "my legs folded under me, and I sat down in the sopping grass. I couldn't understand why I was crying so hard.

"Then I remembered that I had never cried for my father's death.

"My mother hadn't cried either. She had just smiled and said what a merciful thing it was for him he had died, because if he had lived he would have been crippled and an invalid for life . . . he would rather have died than had that happen.

"I laid my face to the smooth face of the marble and howled my loss into the cold salt rain."

The repression and denial of grief seemed helpful at the time even though an overt expression of grief would have been the most natural and healthy response. However, it was only a matter of time before the repression and denial demanded its price. Sylvia Plath's life was troubled repeatedly with emotional illness. At age 30 she ended it with suicide.

Sylvia Plath did not need to hear what a "merciful thing" it was for her father to die. To a child of eight years who loves and needs a father, there can be *no* thankfulness for his death. What she *did* need was to express the multitude of feelings which welled up within her as a result of her great loss. But she was not allowed to mourn.

Certainly there is much to be said in favor of bravery and courage. But when you lose, you do not *need* to "be brave"; what you probably need is to cry and go to pieces.

But the pressure to mask feelings is great. Sometimes it is only in the privacy of my office in the hospital that people feel free to express their manifold feelings of grief over the death of their loved one. They have the notion that it would really be in "bad taste" to let go of their feelings at the bedside of the deceased, or in the hall, or for that matter, anywhere in public. It would be embarrassing to them because they believe that such behavior would be negatively evaluated by virtually everyone who observed them. And the sad part of it is, they are probably right.

My hope is that this book may make a change in that observation. Hopefully by looking in the chapters that follow at some of the more prominent feelings which are experienced in grief over loss we can come to an understanding and acceptance of the wisdom and health inherent in allowing those feelings to have appropriate expression.

Yes it *is* true that some of the behaviors manifested by grieving people appear to be unreasonable, inappropriate and indeed frightening. Yes it *is* often awkward and embarrassing to relate to grieving people. Yes it *is* more safe, comfortable and acceptable (at the moment) to play the game of "Let's Pretend that Nothing Bad Happened" than to express or allow expression of authentic feelings. But let us endeavor to understand and accept the fact that these are normal and natural human experiences and expressions which happen when people are in grief. People in grief should not need to be afraid to express these things; rather they should be supported and encouraged to do so particularly if they believe they will be judged by others if they do.

Crying does not brand a griever as being weak and without faith. Experiencing and expressing feelings of anger in grief may be very appropriate and does not necessarily make one a "bad" person. Idealization and rationalization about the death of a loved one may be quite natural and helpful. Having feelings of guilt does not necessarily judge one as having been negligent or irresponsible to the loved one.

In my observation it is quite appropriate to ascribe the phrase "going to pieces" to this conglomeration of elements common to the experience of grief. Likewise in my observation it is equally appropriate to maintain that such "going to pieces" is the very thing that will hold the griever together as a whole and integrated person. Openly accepting and expressing the feelings of those elements of the grieving process will indeed help maintain emotional and spiritual health and wholeness as one faces and deals with loss.

3

Oh No!

The anesthesia of shock
Denial, fantasy, and reality

I had followed the black 1950 Mercury all the way
down the back road into the trailer court. Three times
I had given them the horn to get their attention and
they still hadn't responded. I knew it was Harry and
Marty Cook in the car—it had to be. Who else would
be driving their car back that road into the trailer
court? I hit the horn again. But still no recognition
from them.

Harry Cook and I were classmates in seminary. He
and Marty had been married about as long as Marilyn
and I. She was a nurse and Marilyn taught school.
They were both Ph.Ts—*P*utting *H*ubby *T*hrough
(school). For over a year we had lived in house trailers
(or mobile homes as they're called now) just four
spaces apart in the trailer court. We had shared good
and not-so-good times together, helped each other in
many ways, and felt really close.

This was not like the Cooks though. I was sure that

they knew it was we who were behind them. So when the black Mercury stopped in front of their trailer, we slowly passed it and I gave them a good blast on the horn; but still . . . no response from them.

I drove on and pulled up in front of our trailer. Marilyn and I got out of the car and as we did I saw a man walking towards us from the Cook's car. But it wasn't Harry; it was another classmate, Tom Connor. Now my curiosity was really up and I called something nonsensical to him as he approached us.

He didn't reply. In fact he didn't do much of anything except continue to walk toward us and look at me. He was acting strangely and I guess I wanted to lighten things up a little. So when he got up to us I asked him what the heck he was doing in Harry Cook's car with Harry Cook's wife. At first he just stood there, and then very quietly he said to me, "Harry is dead."

It was a warm afternoon; quite warm in fact. But there was a sudden hot flush deep into my skin moving quickly over my whole body that had nothing to do with the temperature of the air.

I remember also a feeling of hollowness in my stomach and a lightness about my body and head. I have since experienced that same feeling when I have been aware of being extremely anxious, feeling almost overwhelmed with anxiety.

This all happened very quickly; and in the breath

of a forced laugh I said almost immediately to Tom, "Aw come on; that's a terrible thing to joke about."

"It's no joke," he said; "it's true. Harry is dead."

He said more than that. He said something about underwater accident, drowning, not drowning, aqua lung, he died at the hospital. I really do not remember what he said. I just remember that he was talking as the three of us slowly walked to the trailer.

For some reason I felt hesitant to see Marty; it was as though I was afraid to see her, and yet I wanted to. And then I knew why. For as soon as I stepped inside the trailer and I looked at her and she looked at me, I knew at once that it was all true.

The traumatic news of loss delivers a powerful shock. It is like a hot object or a "live" electrical wire; the human being instinctively draws back from it. A built-in "anesthetic" seems to engulf the griever. Sometimes people pass out and faint. Seeing or hearing of grave loss, a person may faint. It is not unusual. It is as though the brain says to the body, "This is just too much for us; let's get out of here." Fainting or passing out is a very adequate way of "getting out of here"—of getting away from something intolerable or avoiding unbearable pain.

The anesthetic effect usually gives an immediate feeling of numbness—the person feels stunned, as though he or she had been hit in the head. There are feelings of bewilderment, helplessness, disassociation, confusion, depersonalization. The griever seems to be drifting somewhere between reality and fantasy, not really sure which is which.

This feeling of numbness acts as a sort of shock-absorber—a pillow, a softener of the blow. Its function is to protect the griever and to allow him/her to adapt to the situation and do what must be immediately done.

Those who observe grievers in this initial shock see them as somewhat detached, acting without apparent emotion, dealing quite matter-of-factly with the events immediately following the bad news, and sometimes even seeming to have no sense of what is really happening. We are often amazed at how efficiently they operate; in fact, others may actually appear to be more upset by the news than the grievers themselves. And then we say something like, "Oh it's just that the full impact hasn't hit them yet."

Undoubtedly the greatest human defense against that which is intolerable is denial. Here we see how unable the human being is to accept quickly or easily the undesirable, the unacceptable, the distasteful bad news of loss.

The anesthetic effect of the shock of the trauma begets denial. There is a struggle between fantasy and reality. The griever unconsciously says, "It is not true. What I have seen or heard is not true. I did *not* lose it because I do not *want* to lose it."

It is very important to remember that denial is virtually universal to the experience of grief. It goes without saying that no one welcomes the bad news of loss

—indeed not; we want to avoid it. So we flatly deny it. Denial is as natural to grief as laughter is to a funny story. When you hear a funny story, you laugh. When you hear the bad news of loss, you flatly deny it. "Oh no!" That is one phrase expressed by virtually everyone who experiences a loss. Or else we say something like, "I can't believe it"; "I don't believe it"; "There must be some mistake"; "Are you sure you have the right person? report? etc.?" Disbelief reigns. To deal with the trauma we run into the fantasy land of denial, and for a time, reject reality because it is just too much to bear.

The power and strength of denial to resist the reality of loss is, literally, fantastic. Sometimes for a variety of reasons grievers will push the denial to unbelievable limits, flatly discounting the obvious. "I don't want him to be dead; I can't stand that he is dead; he can't be dead; therefore he *isn't* dead, he is alive." This is sometimes the way the logic (or illogic) works. This strong denial seems to be particularly true when there has been no visual confirmation of the death of the loved one because the body was never recovered or was perhaps mutilated beyond visual identification.

Sometimes grievers may deny the death of the loved one through an identification with the deceased, in effect saying, "He did not really die, but lives on through me." The griever takes on the dead person's behavior traits, interests, activities, perhaps even the symptoms of the deceased's last illness.

Then too, denial may be seen in hyperactivity. It may manifest itself in the form of extreme busyness, without the sense of loss.

In early grief there may be something like what psychiatry calls a manic-depressive state. It is similar to a roller coaster ride where you cruise along and then plunge down the rails at break-neck speed only to rise up to a level of "high" which is only temporary because you soon thrust downward to another depth, etc.

In early grief there is this sometimes extravagant fluctuation between acceptance of the loss with all its depression, sorrow and darkness, and denial of the loss —running away from it into activity, avoidance, substitution, indeed a kind of mania.

Just one week after our marriage, Marilyn and I were thrust into our first major experience of loss as husband and wife. Returning from our honeymoon in our first car, a 1946 Chevrolet, we were struck from behind by another automobile and "totalled." The accident happened outside a small Maryland town, early in the morning before daybreak. Miraculously we both escaped unhurt; but we were without transportation and with very little cash. In fact, we had barely enough money to purchase bus tickets back to Ohio.

We may have been physically OK, but emotionally we were a couple of wrecks over the loss of our car. By the time all the necessary matters had been completed with the State Highway Patrol it was early morning, about 9 A.M. Our bus was not scheduled to arrive until early afternoon. There was nothing to do but wait—and grieve. So for the balance of the morning and on into afternoon we rode the emotional roller coaster. We bought ourselves a pocket joke book (of all things) and sat down together on someone's front lawn and began to read it. I suspect that we two must have been quite a sight to passers-by in that small Maryland town because I clearly remember how we would be breaking up with laughter over the jokes one minute, then breaking down with tears, crying and bemoaning our loss the next.

At the time of course we were quite unaware of these dynamics of our grief experience; all we knew was that we were experiencing a painful loss and an awful lot of anxiety. We *had* to get away from our loss —we had to deny it because it was too threatening and too frightening. So the joke book provided a ready vehicle for our escape via denial. And yet our situation was too real to avoid; there we were, sitting on that front lawn, waiting "aeons" for a bus, our wreck of a car lying crumpled in the yard of a local car dealer.

Shock and denial form the beginning phase of the process of grief. They are and need to be recognized as integral parts of grief. Shock is healthy and denial is a natural, normal reaction. The relatively brief experience of shock and denial actually helps the griever to begin to adapt to the loss. The shock and denial experience will generally last anywhere from a few minutes to a few days (although it is extremely risky to attach time periods to any aspect of the grieving process). If the denial persists beyond several days it becomes maladaptive and works against rather than for the griever. It is no longer goal-oriented—designed to allow adaptation to the loss and acceptance of it—but becomes pathological and hinders the griever in dealing with the real world. No doubt we have all known grievers who have manifested a prolonged preoccupation with the deceased—people who have demonstrated a need to preserve relics and mementos of the dead person, or keep things exactly as the dead person had left them. There is a pathological inability to let go of the deceased. The griever believes that sooner or later the lost loved one will come home.

The loss of his wife through death was unbearable for Mr. Lindstrom, so he refused to believe it. Long after her death he continued to call home from his office three or four times a day, letting the telephone ring at least a dozen times. The house of course was empty and he knew that intellectually, but he still hoped that his wife would answer the phone.

If denial persists beyond several days it may be an indicator of a chronic and pathological grief experience. But just as soon as I have said this, I must turn right around and say that acceptance of a loss is not necessarily the *only* and the ultimately desirable way of handling it. In other words, I believe that it is possible that *denial* may be the only way people are able to cope with and handle their loss. I know this is an extremely sensitive area and is therefore vulnerable to misinterpretation. Nevertheless I believe that there are indeed individuals who can only cope with their loss by denying it. Denial may be their only defense; and to take that away from them may cause them to disintegrate and become unable to live their normal daily lives. For some people who use denial it may not appreciably affect their routine living. And we may very well be imposing *our* need upon them if we demand, however "nicely," that they quit their unrealistic denial and finally face reality. If denial is indeed their only way of handling their loss, such an approach as this may be destructive or severely damaging. The hard part of this matter of course lies in the assessment of the personality of the griever. Who are the ones who are truly dependent upon denial as their only way of handling their loss, and who are the ones who are only prolonging the natural grief reaction of denial and thus impeding the natural grief process?

This may very well be a difficult problem. And all I really want to do is to discourage people from just willy-nilly rushing in at grieving people in their early days of grief, immediately endeavoring to set them straight in their thinking and encouraging them to "accept reality" and get out of their fantasy. Rather, let us try to accept grievers in their denial of their loss—to accept how difficult it is for them to accept the loss. Let us empathize with them in that agony of accepting something which is totally unacceptable, and feel with them in wanting to deny it. Through this acceptance of their denial we may be better able to walk slowly with them into an authentic acceptance of the loss.

There is nothing to be gained by supporting a griever's false hopes and misperceptions of reality. Grievers generally believe that their loss is really just a bad dream and that in time it will pass. The prolongation of such wishful thinking is bad enough in the griever, but if it is reinforced by others, the problem is only compounded. It is not only false, but destructive to deny that death has brought a profound separation.

What is helpful to grievers is to encourage them to talk—to talk through their experience of the loss—and then *to listen*. It is helpful to encourage the griever to talk about the lost loved one—to dwell upon the image of the dead person—to remember and review perhaps over and over again the times and experiences they shared in the past. It is often helpful also for the griever to relate repeatedly the events surrounding the death of the loved one. Opportunities for this may occur frequently in the funeral parlor as friends come to "pay their respects." True, this may be a tiring, even exhausting experience for the griever, but it does help in the gradual acceptance of the reality of the loss. Little by little there is the realization and acceptance that from now on the dead person will be absent from the griever's life. It is no longer possible to share the life of the dead person, and there is frankly nothing to be gained by wishing that the deceased were still alive, for it *is* only a wish. Only when this void in the griever's life has been both intellectually and emotionally accepted by the griever can steps be taken to begin to fill that void.

4

Cry Baby, Cry

The outlet of weeping

Our steps were slow as we walked from the Cooks' trailer to our own. As I recall, Marilyn said nothing to me and I said nothing to her. For the moment the denial of Harry's death was gone and the waves of deep sorrow were beginning to break over us.

I opened the door to our trailer and we both walked inside. We still said nothing, mostly because at that moment we didn't need words to communicate. We took each other in our arms and held each other tightly; and then we broke down and sobbed violently over the loss of our dear friend.

Our crying did not last too long, but it was severe. And that was OK. We both felt alright about it. And that too was good because we were able thus to "minister" to each other—to be each other's therapist, if you will. The crying provided each of us with an initial catharsis—a cleansing of the wound that had been created by the loss of our dear friend.

Just what the anatomical connection is between the psychological pain of sorrow and the physiological act of crying, I do not know, if indeed there is one. I do remember reading in a journal where a doctor had said, ". . . tear ducts were given to us by God to express our sorrow."

I don't know what factual basis the doctor had for that statement, but I do know that I agree with it. By experience alone it is evident that crying is a very direct and immediate therapy for emotional or physical pain. Weeping is an expression of our deepest, innermost feelings. And yet, let's face it, in our culture and society, crying is generally regarded as *a sign of weakness*.

If you suspect that that assessment is an overstatement, consider the following observations:

(1) Traditionally, crying is acceptable in children (more so in little girls and less so in little boys), but should be laid aside as the youngster passes through puberty into so-called adulthood. In other words, in the age of maturity, crying is inappropriate.

(2) Traditionally, crying has tended to be more acceptable in women and less acceptable (if at all acceptable) in men. However foolish, the reason generally given was that women are more weak and fragile and crying seems more appropriate to that characteristic. Whereas men, again however foolish, are stronger and more courageous and crying seems quite inappropriate

to that characteristic. Drama, I believe, bears this out notably well; weeping male figures are noticeably few.

(3) People generally apologize for their crying as though their crying was offensive and thus needed apology. People who visit my office for pastoral counseling often become aware of many new feelings as we talk and explore together; and some of those feelings evoke tears. Almost invariably, even there in the intimacy of a counseling relationship, whether man or woman, the person will apologize with words like, "Oh, I'm sorry," or "I really shouldn't break down like that."

(4) Many people of religious orientation view crying over loss as a lack of faith or trust, or lack of hope. They seem to maintain that religious faith and tears are incompatible; that a faith in God and belief in life after death make crying and grieving quite inappropriate. There is the subtle but strong suggestion that if grievers experience such feelings coming on they would be wise to suppress them and thus witness to the strength of their faith.

(5) Then too there are many people who are intelligent, educated and sophisticated who believe that crying is beneath their dignity. A woman once said to me, "Crying is OK for others, but I believe I should be above it. I know it's a release, but it is a rather undesirable display of emotion." This woman liked to believe that she carried the image of a strong person,

which indeed she did; therefore she was convinced that she must be "above" crying. To her, crying would hurt her image.

It is obvious, I think, that here we are up against a formidable barrier to healthy grief work. Because of the fact that our society generally regards crying as a sign of weakness, grievers are reluctant to cry. Because of the fact that our society generally regards stoicism as a sign of courage, grievers are encouraged to "keep a stiff upper lip" and "bear up."

Besides all this, crying people are an embarrassment to most people and they don't know what to do with them or what to say to them. Many people feel awkward with grievers. Like the title of Berne's book, *What Do You Say After You Say Hello?,* what do you say after you say "You have my sympathy"? There is a felt absence of "accepted" protocol. The actual reality of this is sometimes very evident in the atmosphere of funeral parlors when friends come to "pay their respects."

Grievers who are crying and are embarrassing other people are ripe candidates for sedation. Sedatives may indeed help to hold grievers together in their experience of shock and weeping; they may help them maintain a calm and composed appearance and thus win the commendation of society. However, such chemically induced composure may artificially extend the numbness and denial that grief naturally brings and interfere with the health-restoring process of grief work.

Crying, sobbing people may not only embarrass others they may also frighten them; and the others will want to make them stop crying so they won't be so frightened. Again, a sedative will do the trick very well. A sedative will very nicely persuade the griever to stop being so frightening with his crying and sobbing. This is usually more effective than a mere verbal suggestion, although a verbal suggestion can be as powerful, depending upon how much guilt the person making the suggestion places on the griever for his crying, or how much the griever respects the person making the suggestion or wants to please that person.

This whole business of being governed by others' expectations makes for serious difficulty in the grieving process. Grievers who worry about what people will say end up being their own worst enemy, truly working against themselves. No doubt we are all familiar with situations similar to the account of the young woman who tried to "protect" her seven-year-old daughter at the time of her husband's death. Well-meaning friends told her not to cry in front of her daughter because such an outburst might emotionally damage the impressionable little girl. This sounded like good advice to the woman so throughout the grief experience she behaved stoically and managed to suppress her natural feelings over the loss of her husband. Then one day not too long after the funeral, with no provocation whatsoever, this seven-year-old child said to her mother, "How come you didn't love Daddy?" Dumbfounded, the woman asked her daughter where on earth she ever got an idea like that. Her reply was, "You're glad that Daddy died, aren't you? You never cried at all."

The consequence of the young widow's stoicism couldn't have been more clearly defined. She had almost ended up doing precisely what she had expected to avoid. The daughter she had hoped to "save" ended up saving *her*. Once she was brought to realize the foolishness and danger of her suppression of feelings, the woman broke down; and she and her little daughter cried together, finally beginning to launch into their grief work, to mourn the loss of their husband and father.

People who suppress the natural flow of tears in the midst of grief because they believe that others will scorn them need to realize deep in their hearts the truth of that old axiom which says, "You cannot please everyone." Even if your behavior pleases the majority you still have to contend with the criticism of the minority.

The point is you really have nothing to lose and much to gain by allowing yourself to be yourself. The deep feelings of sorrow over loss well up and want to spill out in tears and moanings. In such expression there is healing. Rather than being seen as opposites of each other, tears and courage need to be seen as close relatives to each other. Courage is to face straight-forwardly the pain and sorrow of loss, and to deal with it; courage is not to suppress it and mask it with a phony facade of fortitude.

Furthermore, crying does not deny religious faith or trust or strength. In orthodox Christianity the expression of grief through the shedding of tears has strong support. Crying is not equated with lack of faith. Indeed Jesus himself is reported to have broken down and cried outside the grave of his good friend Lazarus. Jesus who was certainly a well integrated person apparently saw no shame in tears, but simply allowed to happen what normally and naturally *will* happen in the experience of grief over loss.

St. Augustine, who was one of the outstanding fathers of the Christian church tells how he struggled with this matter at the time of the death of his mother, Monica. In Book IX, Chapter XII of his *Confessions* he writes:

> I closed her eyes; and there flowed a great sadness into my heart, and it was passing into tears, when mine eyes at the same time, by the violent control of my mind, sucked back the fountain dry, and woe was me in such a struggle! But, as soon as she breathed her last, the boy Adeodatus burst out into wailing, but, being checked by us all, he became quiet. In like manner also my own childish feeling, which was, through the youthful voice of my heart, finding escape in tears, was restrained and silenced. For we did not consider

it *fitting* to celebrate that funeral with tearful plaints and groanings.

He then goes on to describe the struggle which took place within himself, how he was angry with his human nature which encouraged him to weep, and which he had to wilfully suppress.

Still, in his suppression he found no peace. Only finally in the expression of his grief through tears did he find relief for his soul. He continues: ". . . it was pleasant to me to weep in Thy sight, for her and for me, concerning her and concerning myself. And I set free the tears which before I suppressed, that they might flow at their will, spreading them beneath my heart and it rested in them . . . (I) wept for my mother during a small part of an hour—that mother who had for many years wept over me that I might live in Thine eyes."

As long as St. Augustine was successful in fighting off the tears, he believed he was socially appropriate and doing the right thing; but the price he paid for that "propriety" was inner agony. It was in weeping that he found true comfort and restoration.

Crying is probably the expression of grief which most vividly illustrates my image of grieving as "going to pieces." I know in my own experiences of grief this is precisely how I felt. When I drove home from the hospital where our baby son had died, I was crying so hard I could barely see where I was driving. But

I *needed* to cry; there was nothing else at that time that could have taken the place of deep sobbing. It provided a release for the agonizing pain of my loss. Even though it exhausted me physically it gave relief to my pain.

And I have seen the same thing experienced by scores of people to whom I have ministered in their grief. They broke down and went to pieces, but this very thing was what helped hold them together and kept them from falling apart. I have knelt on the floor beside a young man who was himself on the floor, clutching the bed on which his dead mother lay. He sobbed and wailed and moaned her death. And this was in the Coronary Care Unit of the hospital. I have sat or stood or paced with relatives in the Intensive Care Lounge as they cried out their feelings of loss of a loved one. More than once I have stood in the corridor with a woman who had just lost her husband, she clutching my jacket and burying her face in my shirt front sobbing bitter tears of pain, and I holding her tightly, feeling the inner thrashing of her agony.

I am aware that behaviors such as these are quite upsetting and disturbing to some observers. And I have witnessed many such observers who wanted to persuade the griever who was going to pieces to "pull yourself together." But I have consistently encouraged grievers to allow to happen what they felt inside needed to happen——to let the tears flow and let the healing of mourning take place.

It is important, I believe, to bear in mind that not all grievers cry alike. This is undoubtedly obvious, but probably needs reiterating. Crying may be manifested in uncontrolled sobs and wailings, but crying may also be manifested in quiet, gentle tears. The manner of crying is determined solely by the personality of the individual suffering the loss; otherwise it is inauthentic. Some people are by their nature more "emotional," more vivid in their expression of feelings; others are less so. There is obviously no one way or "right" way to cry in expressing grief over a loss. The griever allows an expression of feeling that is appropriate to him; and for some it is one way, and for others another.

The important thing is that it be *allowed to happen*. What with the internal and external inhibitors to such expression of grief being what they are, I believe that grievers need all the support and encouragement we can give them.

To cry is OK. To cry is helpful. To cry is healing.

5

Why Didn't I . . . ?

Guilt and self-recrimination

I doubt that anyone passes through the experience of grief without feeling some degree of guilt. I know it is a risky thing to make sweeping generalizations like that, but guilt does seem to be universal among grievers.

"There is something I should have done and did not do; or else there is something I should not have done and did do." This is the perception of the griever, and the conclusion is, "Therefore, I feel guilty." And that is precisely accurate, for without going into the matter of guilt in great depth it is still very clear that it has a lot to do, if not everything to do with the "shoulds" and "oughts" of life.

The subject matter of guilt will vary from person to person because our shoulds and oughts are pretty private and individual. But the existence of guilt (or perhaps I should say the potential for the existence of guilt) is present in all of us, that is unless we have succeeded in totally anesthetizing our consciences. And when a person experiences the traumatic loss of a loved one by death, the potential for guilt is realized, and the existence of guilt becomes particularly felt, oftentimes at its utmost. The reason for this lies clearly in the fact of the ultimate finality of death. Let me illustrate.

My father and mother both died when I was a little boy, and the lot of rearing me fell to my aunt (my mother's sister) and her husband. For all intents and purposes my aunt and uncle were my mother and father although they never legally adopted me.

I believe my experience at home growing up was normal and "usual." At age 18 I left home for the university, and at 22 made the separation complete by getting married.

During the years that followed I wrote, I visited, I telephoned my aunt and uncle with what I believed to be reasonable frequency. But I was aware that they would have liked my communication and contact to have been *more* frequent. And I would say to myself, "I really should write or phone and visit more often." And then I would go about my business saying, "Oh well, next week, or next month, or next summer."

My uncle died in 1968. And then it was too late.

I remember that it was during his funeral service that the feeling of guilt descended most heavily upon me, and I cried hot tears of regret. Much as I might have *wanted* to write him or call him or visit him, I could no longer. "Why didn't I . . . ?" "I wish I had. . . ." "If only I had. . . ."

I tried to deal with my feeling of guilt logically and rationally. Had I really done anything *wrong?* I hadn't abandoned him. I hadn't been disrespectful. I hadn't caused him shame. I had kept in touch. I had "done my duty," whatever that meant.

But it was all no good. No matter what I came up with it made no sense or it was *not enough;* there was always more I *could* have done, and I didn't. I doubt that I could have come up with anything that would have satisfied and eased my feeling of guilt. In fact, I know that I would not have been able to do that.

This, I have learned, is characteristic of the guilt associated with the experience of grief. There is very little, if any logic to it and it is never satisfied by explanation. Grievers themselves usually create it and give it its power; and there is nothing they can do (they are powerless) to correct the situation with the deceased because the deceased is dead—it is too late.

In the experience of loss by death grievers are faced with an absolute, unalterable, irreversible situation; there is nothing they can do to, for or about that relationship. True, grievers can build monuments, give memorials or offer special prayers for the dead loved one; but a direct, personal relationship can no longer be. And *that* is what would be required to alleviate the guilt. But as the saying goes, "What's done is done."

So grievers say, "Why didn't I *tell* him how much

I loved him?" "Why didn't I send her flowers *then?*" "Why did I have to quarrel with him before he left for work this morning?" "Why did I encourage him to take that job?" "Why didn't I *make* her go to the doctor?" "Why did I let her work so hard?"

Grievers ruminate over having failed the deceased in any of a multitude of ways: having argued with, disagreed with, conflicted with, spoken or thought ill of, avoided, been angry with, neglected, disappointed, been unaffectionate toward, grieved, forgotten, estranged, caused pain to, etc.

"Why did I do this or not do that" implies "I should not have done this or I should have done that." This, then, implies, "Maybe if I hadn't done this or had done that, she would not have died and would still be alive for me to be able to do this, that and the other thing."

The profound implication in all this is that grievers see themselves as powerful enough to have saved the life of the deceased!

This is particularly evident in the clinical setting when grievers demonstrate sometimes-severe self-reproach, accusing themselves of negligence and preoccupying themselves with the details preceding the death of the loved one. Even though the death was definitely unavoidable or unpredictable, grievers may believe that somehow it could have been prevented "if only. . . ." Here, the words, "if only" are substituted for "why didn't I?"

"If only I had hired a private duty nurse around the

clock, maybe he wouldn't have died." "If only we had called Doctor X, the specialist. . . ." "If only I hadn't quarreled with him before he left for work this morning. . . ." "If only I hadn't left her bedside to go home. . . ."

This last statement is a very common expression of guilt among grievers in mourning the death of a spouse who died while in the hospital. The spouse may have virtually *lived* in the patient's room for several days and is truly exhausted and in need of rest and refreshment. If the patient should die while the spouse is away from the bedside the spouse may feel deep pangs of guilt and in fact may want to believe that his or her leaving the patient was what was responsible for the death. Hence, "If only I hadn't left her bedside to go home. . . ." Here again is the clear implication that grievers see themselves as powerful enough to have saved the life of the deceased.

Usually there is no logic to the guilt grievers feel. However, this may not always be the case. Sometimes grievers feel guilty quite justifiably and are faced with the dilemma of having the guilt and never being able to have it absolved by the deceased. It is too late for forgiveness from the one offended.

Such a person may find relief by confessing to a trusted friend who will listen in an attitude of acceptance without passing judgment. True sorrow for the offense committed against the deceased may allow the griever to feel forgiveness from even a higher authority, namely God. We *do* live in an atmosphere of God's grace, and his forgiveness *does* rest upon those who confess to him that they are truly sorry for their offenses, even if it is impossible to make amends to the one offended. The person who deals with such a griever needs to be a sensitive person who will neither rush in with reassurance on the one hand nor hold it back on the other.

Something of this same approach is necessary for all of us as we deal with people in grief who are experiencing feelings of guilt. In all probability the griever *will* feel guilt; it may not be logical but it is natural and *real*. The important thing is to accept the reality of it; not to rush in and say, "Oh come now, that's foolish thinking. You know there's no connection between your argument and your husband's death." Or, "Don't be silly. You did everything you could. You don't have to feel guilty about anything."

It may be true that the griever's logic is unsound and he *doesn't* have to feel guilty, but such an approach is not only not helpful but actually generative of more guilt. The griever consciously or unconsciously says to himself, "Gee, I'm doing something foolish, or something I *shouldn't* be doing," and thus feels more guilt than before.

The sensitive response to the griever who feels guilt is to accept the expression of guilt and to say in your own way, "It's OK. It's a natural thing that you should feel guilty. I think it's part of the way we human beings are." To encourage grievers to talk about *how* they believe they failed the deceased, provides an opportunity for them to view more objectively the failings in their relationship, and hopefully to recognize and accept those failings as being part of the unavoidable consequence of being human. Yes, there are regrets; but there probably always will be regrets. To give quick reassurance without hearing out the grievers' "confession" may also increase their feelings of guilt and cause them to believe that you simply do not grasp the magnitude of their failings in the relationship with the deceased.

To empathize with grievers helps them know that it is clear to you that they can feel as they do: "You can't help but think, can you, that there *must* have been something more that you could have done."

It is also helpful, I believe, not only to accept the grievers' guilt and empathize with their feelings, but to reinforce the good things, the positive deeds they did to and for the deceased. Grievers need this kind of appropriate reassurance just as much as they need acceptance of the reality of their guilt feelings. Here in the clinical setting I have been able to say to many grieving widows and widowers, "I can see how hard it is for you to believe that everything that could have been done, was done. You can't help but think that there must have been something else—something that would have saved her. And I think that's normal—that's natural. But I've been here with you, have talked with you, have watched you; and for what it's worth to you, I want you to know that I think you did everything humanly possible—even more than would be expected you should do. I think you can feel OK. And I believe that if your loved one could, she would tell you the same thing."

Like all the dynamics of grief, guilt moves in to the experience of grief in a very natural and real way. Like most of the other dynamics it does not make a lot of sense—it is in fact illogical most of the time. But being able to accept it, to understand it and to deal with it will be an integrating factor in the grief experience, because working through these feelings of guilt the griever may feel a sense of release from the deceased and may thus be further enabled to let go of the lost loved one.

6

Four-letter Words

Anger and Hostility

I was truly frightened. I thought for sure that Martin Johnson was going to hit someone. He paced the floor of the corridor outside his father's room like a caged animal. He had a wild look in his eyes. In his perception, literally no one was doing anything right; there were dozens of people flocking around his father but no one was saving him. And he was furious. He would have liked to have taken the whole company of medical and paramedical "saviors" and thrown them out the window.

Everett Johnson was a widower 82 years old. In recent years he had been troubled with heart problems and now his general condition had become very weak. He had been a patient in our hospital for about ten days, but suddenly on this particular afternoon he had suffered a cardiac arrest. His only child, Martin, had been notified immediately and within half an hour, he was outside his father's room, angrily pacing.

It was only a quarter hour more before Everett Johnson died. When the nursing supervisor informed him, Martin shouted a curse and clenched his fist as though to strike her. He cursed her; he cursed the whole C-arrest team which he described as "vultures," and he cursed doctors in general, whom he described as "butchers and thieves." He personified the entire hospital as being incompetent and irresponsible; we could be accused of false advertising he said, because we claim to heal people when in fact we let them die. He called me a phony leech and said that I and my "lovey God" could both go to hell.

Martin Johnson raved on and on condemning, threatening and cursing; but gradually the power of his rage appeared to wane and he began to show signs of physical and emotional exhaustion. Very gently and carefully I suggested to him that we might go down to a little conference room at the end of the hall and just sit and rest.

"I don't need to rest, and I don't need your help!"

But it was only a few more minutes before he, still angry, snapped, "Where is this place?"

We walked down the carpeted hall silently. He was quiet in body as well. When we entered the room he sat down in a chair at the small conference table. I closed the door and sat opposite him. In a moment he folded his arms on the table, let his head fall into them and began to sob violently, moaning, "Oh my God, my God."

In the time we spent together, Martin Johnson vividly described the depth of agony he felt over the loss of his father. To Martin, his father was a very "valuable" loved one about whom he had cared deeply all his life, and who now, was gone from him. He began to apologize for his behavior and verbalized a keen sense of shame for the way he had acted saying that that wasn't like him at all. I accepted his apology and empathized as best I could with his pain of loss and anger about it. I told him that I believed that we could all handle that alright, but that if he wanted to apologize to anyone else on the staff he certainly could. Then I asked him if he would like to see his father before we began to make the necessary arrangements with funeral director, etc., and he said he would. So we got up and slowly walked down the hall to Everett Johnson's room. And Martin Johnson began to say good-bye to his father.

Martin Johnson's story is indeed a dramatic one. But not everyone expresses anger and hostility as he did. Anger *may be* expressed loudly and dramatically, strongly and overtly; but anger can be just as valid and authentic when it is expressed quietly and subtly.

When Margaret Wolfe's sister Marie, died, Margaret was left with a great burden of responsibility. The two women were both in their fifties and had remained unmarried all their lives. They had both stayed at home to "look after" their mother who seemed to *need* looking after from the time that their father died, early in their lives. Their mother had become invalid and senile over the years, but the two women shared the responsibility of continuing to take care of her at home.

When Marie became ill and had to be hospitalized, Margaret was very much concerned about her and about the responsibility of taking care of their mother. Marie's illness was severe and her prognosis poor. Her condition worsened and despite all efforts, she died.

Margaret was very stoic about the loss. She wept gently, but was quite "responsible" for herself. Before she left the hospital, Margaret and I went together into her sister's room; Margaret wanted to see her one last time before the funeral parlor. The two of us stood side by side at her dead sister's bed. Margaret looked intently at her sister's face; and then quietly, but with a definite tinge of bitterness, said, "Now, I'll have to take care of her all by myself."

The burden of caring for her mother was now Margaret's responsibility *alone*. And although she loved her sister dearly, she felt abandoned, and was angry with her sister for dying, for "running out" on her, and leaving her alone to care for her mother. Her expression of anger directed toward her sister was quiet and subtle, but very real.

Such quiet and subtle expression of anger by grievers is much more tolerable to observers because it really doesn't even seem to be present. When however, the expression of anger towards the deceased is more dramatic and loud, this kind of behavior may be very disturbing and frightening to observers. In fact, when a griever's expression of anger to the deceased is overt, observers hardly know what to do with him/her. The griever may shout and curse at the deceased, or actually strike the body of the deceased. This type of behavior seems to be out of place entirely or even pathological to the majority of observers, and they tend to rush in to prevent the griever from expressing such feelings. They fail, however, to realize that anger is a very real and reasonable part of the experience of grief. It is normal and natural and as such should be expressed rather than suppressed or repressed, even though the mode of expression seems to them (the observers) to be inappropriate.

Anger in grief may arise from any number of reasons. It may, for instance, come from guilt. At the death of a loved one, I may feel guilty for having failed the deceased—for not having done what I "should" have done, or as *much* as I should have done. But there is no longer any opportunity for me to do it, and I feel frustrated, thwarted, in my wish to atone for my failure. I thus become angry—angry because I am powerless to correct the situation about which I feel guilty.

I may also feel anger over my feeling of helplessness—over my frustration of not knowing "why."

Anger may be resentment specifically towards the deceased. I may resent the deceased for having gone off and left me. Again, there may be no logic or reason to this feeling, but it is nevertheless very real to the griever. When the parent of a young child dies, especially at the time that the child seems to need the parent most, the child experiences resentment towards the parent for having "run out" on him or her. "When I needed you most, you left me!"

The same may be true of a griever's feelings about the death of a spouse, particularly if there are young children involved. The spouse may have strong feelings of resentment right in the midst of the agony of the loss—resentment towards the spouse who has "run out on me and left me to take care of these children all by myself."

The anger of grief is usually a secondary feeling stemming from the feeling of guilt, of abandonment, of the insecurity of being alone. It is illogical in itself and the way it is directed may also be extremely illogical. For instance there was no logic at all to Martin Johnson's anger. The team in the hospital did everything in its power to save the life of his father. He truly had no "right" to be angry with any of us. Nevertheless he was. Anger was a very real feeling for him, and the easiest place for him to project it was onto the staff. Which is not unusual. Grievers often project the anger of their grief to innocent bystanders. *Someone* has *got* to be responsible.

Nor is there usually any logic to being angry at the deceased for dying on you and leaving you stuck with whatever responsibility. Our loved ones do not die on us just to make our lives tough. Intellectually we all know that, but emotionally at the time of grief it may be an altogether different story. Recognizing those feelings of anger and dealing with them is emotionally healthy. Suppressing or repressing them into the unconscious is dangerous because there they never get dealt with but only cause the person emotional difficulty somewhere down the pike.

Sometimes, however, being angry with the deceased loved one *is* justifiable and the griever is truly torn by ambivalence. I knew of a farmer who had been working on his huge tractor and happened to get it into motion while standing in front of the giant rear wheel. It knocked him over and crushed him to death. The pastor who ministered to his widow told me that it was many weeks after the funeral before she was able to identify the feelings of anger which she had towards her husband for being so careless. Having feelings of anger towards her spouse (whom she dearly loved) was so objectionable to her that she promptly repressed them. Her conscious feelings of loss were unconsciously affected by her repressed anger and she continued to be miserable in her grief. When she was able to realize that it was OK to feel anger towards her husband *as well as* feel the terrible pain of having lost her loved one, she was freed from the weight that was holding her back in her grief work. She was able to move on in the grieving process because she was able to accept her ambivalent feelings.

Expressing anger is a frightening thing for many

people, and it seems to take on added awe in the experience of grief over death. "I really shouldn't be angry; I should be able to control myself." "It is unreasonable that I should be angry." "What will people say if I lose my temper, especially at a time like this."

Consequently, many people who will not allow themselves to be angry because it is frightening or because it is believed to be inappropriate will unconsciously turn their anger inward and experience it as depression. Most internalized anger becomes depression, and this is especially convenient for grievers because they feel depressed by the loss anyway. So anger internalized easily adds onto the already existing condition.

Anger may also be directed towards God. Because in the griever's perception God is supposed to be in control of all things he is therefore responsible for the death of the loved one. In the anger of frustration over being powerless to prevent the death of the loved one, grievers may curse God, deny God, blame God, abandon their faith ("Who can believe in a God who would do a thing like this?").

On the other hand, such feelings of anger towards God may be so intolerably unacceptable to grievers because of their religious orientation ("You just don't get angry with God.") that they consciously push them out of their mind or unconsciously repress them.

I mentioned earlier in Chapter 4 how Jesus of Nazareth is reported to have cried at the death of his friend Lazarus. Another feeling expressed at the graveside was the feeling of anger. Mary, Lazarus' sister, confronted Jesus with apparent anger and bitterness brought about by her grief over her brother's death. She said to Jesus, "Lord, if you had been here, my brother would not have died!" And, according to the account Jesus accepted her anger. He neither reproached her nor endeavored to make her stop. He apparently saw it as an appropriate expression of feeling.

For many people in our society however, it is very difficult to accept anger, hostility and resentment as it may be expressed by anyone, not only a grieving person. Angry people are frightening so the tendency is to want to rush in and make them stop being so frightening—and that means that we try to make them abandon their anger. We try to help them with their crooked logic, or tell them that they'll feel better when it's all over, or encourage them to calm down before they have a coronary themselves. In other words, many of us will try to get angry grievers to suppress their feelings of anger and in doing so only encourage more guilt or depression or both within them.

Loss *does* make us angry; and anger is *not* inappropriate to the grieving experience. Anger is a natural and normal part of the experience of grief and needs to be regarded as such. We may feel anger towards the deceased, towards ourselves, or we may project it onto a scapegoat—God or anyone around us. The normal thing is to express the anger—to ventilate that feeling. It usually is a matter of getting it out and getting rid

of it, which is far more desirable than denying or repressing it and letting its emotional energy lie back
in the unconscious building up for some kind of a
breakthrough. It is usually of brief duration. As in the
situation with Martin Johnson, his outburst was short-
lived and it was a prelude to breaking down into tears.
This is not at all an unusual pattern: grievers may un-
load their hostility by exploding in anger or expressing
quiet bitterness, and then immediately break into sobs.
In this demonstration of going to pieces there is genuine healing; and such expression of feeling will help
hold them together as they continue through the grief
process.

7

It Was for the Best

Rationalization— we must have a reason

There are indeed many hard questions in our experience of life, but none probably as difficult, even unfathomable, as those questions raised by loss. The questions grievers ask *sound* simple enough, but they are piercing and complex; they probe the very essence of being; they challenge the private secrecy of the book of life: "Why did it happen?" "Why did it happen to me?" "Why did I lose?" "What is the purpose of this loss?" There is an agony in those questions, and grievers intuitively resent their hardness. They get adamant and demand answers.

Because I am not at this moment grieving myself, I am able to look at this rationally and say that suffering and pain are a part of life. Plain and simply, *that is the way it is;* that is the scheme of things. Maybe not by design but by result (circumstance?) pain and suffering and loss and death are aspects of life as we know it. There is no such thing as a trauma-free existence.

Therefore why are we so unable to accept life as such? Why do we have to find reasons for our losses? Why do we have to explain them?

Perhaps it is power. Perhaps it is the need to be in control. "I refuse to accept this; I demand to know why." Most of us cannot tolerate the unanswered, the un-understood. To us particularly here in western civilization, the mysterious is virtually unbearable. We simply have got to have answers or we will go berserk.

Now there are very few people who will say that, or even admit it to themselves. What most do is to rationalize. Rationalization, according to a not-so-charitable and not-so-technical definition, is simply "to invent answers to unanswerable questions, and to find reasons for unreasonable circumstances." A little more sophisticated definition might be: "the conscious justification of acts, concepts and attitudes after these have been already determined by unconscious motivations." Rationalization is to use only those data which will support a conclusion which you have already decided you want to reach. Facetiously it may be stated thus: "I have already made up my mind; please do not confuse me with the facts."

Because the need for answers appears so strongly, if we cannot come up with the actual answer, reason or explanation, we will create or manufacture one of our own. It may not make much sense to objective observers, but it will satisfy the need. In fact, a lot of the "answers" people come up with through rationali-

zation are nothing more than euphemisms and plati-
tudes. Nevertheless, they do meet the need to explain
and thus make the acceptance of loss more bearable.

Because of the great need for answers and explana-
tions, grievers are bound to do some rationalizing somewhere in the grief process. Sometimes rationalization
is helpful in working through the experience of grief;
it can provide an effective way of coping with the
agony of loss ("I have found a reason; therefore the
pain is more bearable"). Sometimes, however, it is
nothing more than thinly veiled denial which promotes
repression of feelings. Sometimes it enables the griever;
sometimes it disables him.

The "sour grapes" form of rationalization may be
very helpful in handling the grief of loss. This mecha-
nism gets its name from the fable of the "Fox and the
Grapes." In the fable, the fox was unable to reach
the very desirable bunches of grapes, so he handled the
frustration of the experience (the loss) by saying, "Oh
well, they are much too sour to enjoy anyway, so there's
no great loss."

Sour grapes rationalization helps the griever by discounting the value of the lost loved object. In essence
the griever says, "I really haven't lost as much as it
might appear I have lost." There is a tendency here to
consider and stress only the negative or undesirable
characteristics of the lost loved object, almost to the
exclusion of its desirability. If an observer attempts to
point out the desirability of it, the griever will prompt-

ly say, "Yes, but on the other hand. . . ." This works effectively in the loss of a spouse by divorce or separation, the loss of a girlfriend or boyfriend (particularly if you have been jilted), the loss of a job, failure to get a promotion, having to move from your community, etc. What was lost was truly very valuable and desirable, and the griever almost instinctively questions, "Why? Why did I lose?" And the answer of sour grapes rationalization is: "Fret not; for what you lost isn't really worth fretting over." Sour grapes rationalization is rarely that blunt, but that is the essence of how it works its efficacy.

The converse of "sour grapes" is sometimes facetiously called "sweet lemons." It is the Pollyanna rationalization. The Pollyanna approach finds good in everything, therefore this form of rationalization answers the agonizing questions of "Why?" by saying, "It was for the best; and it will work out for the best." This simplistic formula encourages the griever to develop a blind acceptance of the trauma and loss by denial of feelings and to go blithely tripping along to the next trauma.

The words, "It was for the best," may be heard often at the loss of a loved one by death. "She is better off; she is free of her suffering." "It is for the better; God knows what complications might have set in." "She would not have wanted to be a burden."

There may be a category all its own for religious rationalization; God figures prominently in the rationalization of loss (particularly of a loved one by death) and the answering of the "why" questions. In one brief sentence—"It was God's will."—religious rationalization answers all the "why's" and makes the reason for the loss very clear. "God in his wisdom saw fit to do this," and the implication is, "Ours is not to question."

Not only is this fairly common approach distorted theology, it is also, I believe, detrimental to the grieving process. It only discourages grief work. With one broad swipe of the brush the whole loss experience is whitewashed and all issues resolved. It may in fact be downright pathological when it is used to deny and repress the multitude of grief feelings over the loss by explaining the loss with extremely unrealistic reasoning. An example of this was the young father who did this at his baby's death. His wife had delivered twin girls and one of the babies died shortly after birth. The babies' mother was broken up by the loss and grieved openly; but the father calmly rationalized the loss by explaining the death this way: (1) God wanted her in heaven. (2) God wanted to teach us something. (3) God wanted her for research.

This kind and degree of rationalization will definitely work against the griever because it seals off completely any awareness and expression of the feelings of loss. But the dynamic energy of those feelings still remains in the griever's unconscious to trouble him in a variety of ways.

A more helpful way of using rationalization in the

process of grief can be illustrated by the somewhat humorous although seriously stated comment of a griever at her sister's death. Mabel and Ann had lived together virtually all their lives. They were only a year apart in age, neither had ever married, and apparently they were very close to each other over their many years, somewhat like the saying, "Two peas in a pod." Mabel was 83 years old and Ann 82 when Ann was admitted to the hospital. Each woman had taken good care of herself physically, but disease had overtaken Ann and there was little that could be done for her. Mabel stayed faithfully close by during Ann's last days and seemed to quietly accept her death the day Ann died. I stood beside Mabel, who was just a little wisp of a woman, and watched her look gently and lovingly into her dead sister's face. And then she quietly whispered, "Oh, if only she could have had a good B.M., this never would have happened."

Now there was of course no reason or rationality at all to her explanation. Having a "good B.M." would not have saved her sister's life. But really, what difference did that make? This little 83-year-old lady used a simple, innocent rationalization to help herself handle her feelings of grief over the loss of her dear sister. And I hugged her for it.

Every crisis contains within it the potential for a positive growth experience on the part of all who are affected by it. The key word here is of course, "potential." The experience of loss may be not only undesirable, it may feel like an encounter with bold-faced evil. Nevertheless we know that it is *possible* to emerge from the experience having grown in strength and wholeness. This is not to employ the old cliché which says of a hard experience, "You'll be a better person for it." Nor is it to reinforce the Pollyanna approach which encourages grievers to skip cheerily through the tragedy of loss, kidding themselves into denying feelings. Rather it is realistic rationalization, which sees the experience of loss as presenting the possibility of a turning point in life—a turn for *better* as well as a turn for worse. To focus on that possibility is a positive aid in working through the process of grieving a loss. I have seen this particularly manifested in the lives of men who have lost their jobs, especially at a critical point in their lives. Virtually all see the loss of job as an evil thing, causing all kinds of agony and typical feelings of grief. Some, however, in working through their feelings, recognize that this loss can be a kind of catalyst that breaks up old ruts, rattles old habits and pressures the griever to map out new ways and paths.

There is in loss the potential for enriching one's own personality and for experiencing a more fulfilling and rewarding life. This is no rose-colored, Pollyanna vision —it is authentic possibility. And if the griever acts on it, it can become reality.

8

He Was a Good Man

Idealization and selective memory

> Mem'ries, may be beautiful, and yet,
> What's too painful to remember
> We simply choose to forget.

The songwriters were absolutely right when they wrote those words into the song *The Way We Were*. They are talking about a thing called "selective memory"—idealization. Remember the *good* old days? Well, just how *good* they were may be questionable; but that is what we generally remember. We select out the good and we tend to idealize the past.

Grievers usually practice idealization too; it is rather common to the grief experience. Sometimes it even has its own humor. Let's say that Joe has died and his widow Helen is meeting and talking with friends who have come to the funeral parlor to "pay their respects." Most everyone knew Joe to be a relatively anti-social person. He drank rather heavily and appeared to stay away from home as much as he reasonably could. He tended to be self-centered and seemed to be motivated to help others only if there was some pay-off in it for him. From time to time he would rough up Helen to remind her that he was still in charge.

One night he got into a fist-fight in a bar and was rather badly shaken up by it. When he left the bar he stepped out into the street in somewhat of a daze and unwittingly stepped in front of a passing truck. The truck knocked him down and ran over him, and Joe was crushed to death.

Teary-eyed, Helen would tell the story over and over to the visitors in the mortuary. And each time she would look into the face of the body in the casket and say, "Ah, he was a good man. He was a good husband and a good father. He took good care of us and provided for us well." And the visitors, mildly astonished at such commentary, would look into the casket to be sure it was the same Joe they knew. From Helen's eulogy it sounded like a different man.

Why did Helen choose to say what she did? Why didn't she say, "Joe was a mean man who caused us and others much anguish. I'm not particularly glad he's dead, but I am glad that we're free of him." Is it only the more or less natural tendency towards selective memory that causes idealization, or is there also something of that old taboo of speaking ill of the dead that feeds into idealization?

It is good manners to respect the dead. We don't

speak ill of them and we don't walk on their graves. I remember vividly walking through the cemetery one day with my mother. At nine years of age I wasn't particularly careful where I was walking. My mother got angry with my carelessness and told me that I shouldn't walk on people's graves. I asked her why not. And all she answered was, "It isn't nice."

It is difficult to know how these things get started. Perhaps it has something to do with the "old days" before the time of burial vaults. Graves used to settle long after the burial. Maybe someone stepped on a "settling" grave one day and sunk down into it and fractured an ankle. And that was how "You shouldn't walk on graves" got started. Or maybe it *is* only a matter of respect.

And why shouldn't we speak ill of the dead? Is that only a matter of respect? Or is this a vestige of old superstition which supposes that the spirit of the dead one will haunt you if you speak ill of the departed. Someone told me once that we should not speak ill of the dead because they are unable to defend themselves. And that is certainly true.

But whatever, grievers continue to idealize those whom they have lost through death, sorting out and forgetting the not-so-good things and recalling only the good. As the song says, "What's too painful to remember, we simply choose to forget." Grievers have a *need* to idealize.

A pastor friend of mine told me of an experience in

his parish which involved the death of a member in the midst of an illicit love affair. The man had suffered a fatal coronary while with another woman in a motel room. The woman had notified the police and the police had asked him, the pastor, to accompany them to the home of the man's widow to break the news to her. Upon hearing the news, he said, she went to pieces sobbing. She wanted to know nothing of the incident in the motel, and only praised her husband for his goodness and honor. To the best of his knowledge, the pastor said, she has not yet come to grips with the fact of her husband's infidelity. She is also, according to his description, a somewhat neurotic woman.

"What's too painful to remember, we simply choose to forget." This was her way of handling an intolerable experience of reality.

Something of this was true of the woman whom I mentioned in chapter 6 whose husband was killed beneath his tractor. In the idealization of him she conveniently "forgot" his carelessness and her anger over it. She regained her balance, so to speak, only when she was able to deal consciously with that assessment of him and her feelings about it.

Perhaps grievers are reluctant to speak ill of the dead most of all because of the fear of what people will say. If Helen *were* to stand at Joe's casket and say, "Joe was a mean man who caused us and others much anguish; I'm glad we're free of him," the visitors would probably be just as astonished as they are with her idealization. They may know it is true; but Helen isn't supposed to say that. Helen *shouldn't* say that. The rule of the game is that if you can't say something good about a person then you shouldn't say anything at all; particularly if the person happens to be dead. There is definitely societal and cultural pressure involved here; to speak ill of the dead is definitely considered to be in very bad taste. Even politicians who have condemned a fellow politician for a legion of "crimes" will change their assessment of him should that politician die. Charges and countercharges are part of the game of politics; but death changes the rules.

Idealization of the lost loved one is clearly a common part of the experience of grief. In a way, one may consider idealization to be the opposite of sour grapes rationalization, even though both seek to accomplish the same purpose. Whereas sour grapes rationalization endeavors to help the griever deal with loss by discounting the desirable aspects of the lost loved object, idealization seeks to accomplish the same thing by "forgetting" the *un*desirable aspect.

Again, as in the case with denial, there is nothing to be gained by rushing in to "correct" a griever's idealization and "help" him or her to be more realistic. Nor on the other hand is it particularly helpful to reinforce the idealization, particularly if it appears in a distorted form. The helpful attitude is one of empathy, accepting the griever's idealization as a way of handling the pain of loss. It is a natural thing—it is a need—to bury with the deceased those undesirable and painful memories. The agonizing pain of separation is bad enough; who wants bad memories on top of it?

But we should also try to be sensitive to any indications given by grievers that they might want to deal with some negative, unpleasant matters or feelings concerning the deceased. We can accept that too. We need to be particularly sensitive to those who are using idealization only because it is a societal expectation and are consciously suppressing other feelings. Finding a non-judgmental listener is one of the greatest discoveries any griever can make.

9

Fidgets and Fuzziness

Restlessness
and circular thinking

Karen Brown and her brother George were both present when their father died. Now they were in the Intensive Care lounge of the hospital waiting for other relatives to arrive. Both people were the "strong—silent" type; they were relatively quiet in expressing inner thoughts and feelings. Both people were also quite large in build.

George Brown began to map out a course between chair A, the window, and chair B. He would walk rapidly from chair A to the window, look out briefly, heave a deep sigh and walk briskly to chair B. He would sit down, drum his fingers on his knees, get up and walk quickly to chair A, where he would sit down and cross his right leg over his left, then his left leg over his right, heave a deep sigh, get up and walk rapidly to the window and repeat the pattern. With minor variations, George Brown kept this movement up until the other relatives arrived.

Meanwhile, his sister Karen was seated in another chair, a large and heavy armchair with a relatively broad base. She said nothing and only looked straight ahead. She began to rock her body in the chair. Then in rhythmic movement her rocking became harder and harder. She held onto the arms of the chair tightly. Soon the whole chair was rocking, tipping back with front legs off the floor then tipping forward with back legs off the floor. She was so engrossed that I truly do not believe she was even aware that she was in motion.

To the casual observer such behavior may seem strange, or at least wasteful of precious energy. The casual observer may want to move in and say, "Listen George, why don't you sit down and try to relax a little, and save some of that energy that you're going to be needing in the days ahead."

But despite the seeming wisdom of such advice, that is not what George (or his sister Karen) needs at that time. What each of them needs is to work off the restless energy which their experience of grief is generating within them in the manner which they rather naturally fall into. For George it was pacing; for Karen, rocking.

People in grief may very well experience feelings of restlessness and become highly agitated. They may develop rocking patterns, they may pace the floor, they may stand up—sit down—stand up—sit down, they may drum their fingers, they may bite their nails.

The activity of their restlessness may be highly rit-
ualized, or on the other hand it may be quite aimless.
Sometimes the person simply cannot sit quietly or sit
still, and will move about without any apparent direction, manifesting purposeless activity, seemingly search-
ing for something to do. Often there is a respiratory
involvement, and the person sighs deeply, or yawns,
or simply feels "hungry for air."

The inner agitation of the anxiety of the loss may
be active at night as well as in the day. The griever
may awaken at night and feel compelled to get up and
get out of bed and walk about the room, heaving deep
sighs all the while. Insomnia is a common characteristic of the grieving process; statistically 85 percent of
people in grief have trouble sleeping. Grievers experience weariness and exhaustion—everyday functions
seem to become chores. Although there seems to be a
lot of restless energy it is often a real drudgery to do
what must be done.

This experience seems to help cause a decrease in
interest in the affairs of daily life and work. The griever tends to become somewhat withdrawn, detached,
apathetic. There appears to be a loss of interest in
normal pleasures and things which regularly claimed
enthusiastic attention. All combined, these factors make
for a broad and general decline in the griever's desire
for social interaction; he or she tends to become detached.

Along with the inner agitation and restlessness there

is often another dynamic somewhat related—circular thinking. The loss of a loved one definitely affects a person's thought processes. Grievers may be acutely *aware,* but clear thinking very often escapes them. Irrationality sounds sensible. Understandably they tend to follow the path of least resistence; it is so much easier to go around in circles in their thinking than to "move ahead" and map out necessary plans and actions. Grievers find it very difficult to initiate and maintain an organized pattern of activity. They may go through the motions and somehow "make it through the day," but it is not without a great deal of effort.

The griever may have a difficult time remembering the immediate past, what she did or did not do. People become absent-minded in grief. For example, the griever may telephone the same relative a second time to inform him of the death of the loved one, not realizing that she called him just a few minutes before.

There is confusion, and it becomes difficult for grieving people to make decisions. They may go around and around the subject, never really being able to get hold of it well enough to make a decision. It is not at all unusual to hear grievers openly or subtly ask for help in decision-making.

Grief may greatly affect a person's powers of concentration; grievers may find that they are virtually unable to keep their minds on ordinary tasks. Instead of easily being able to concentrate (even on reading something) they find their minds wandering, generally back to some preoccupation with thoughts of the lost loved one.

For such reasons there is a definite impropriety about casually encouraging grievers to "get busy," "get active," "get involved," "keep occupied," and "forget the past." This is virtually impossible for the griever and only demonstrates the impatience and insensitivity of people who are unwilling to understand and empathize with people in grief.

Consider the impossibility of "forgetting the past." The past is an intimate part of the griever. If the relationship with the lost loved one was sufficiently deep and meaningful to warrant genuine grief, then it is clear that a substantial portion of the griever's life was tied into the lost loved one. In *A Grief Observed,* C. S. Lewis vividly recounts his experience of grief over the death of his wife, and speaks to this matter. He says:

> I think I am beginning to understand why grief feels like suspense. It comes from the frustration of so many impulses that had become habitual. Thought after thought, feeling after feeling, action after action, had H. [his wife] for their object. Now that target is gone. I keep on through habit fitting an arrow to the string; then I remember and have to lay the bow down. So many roads lead to H. I set out on one of them. But now there's an impassable frontier-post across it. So many roads once; now so many *culs de sac*.

Restlessness and circular thinking are common dynamics of the experience of grief and need to be accepted as such by grievers and observers alike. Perhaps it is easy to become impatient with the agitation and disorganization of grievers and tempting to want to reprimand them for their "fuzzy" thinking and absentmindedness. But frankly, there is nothing to be gained, but harm to be done, by pushing for quick cures to these symptoms.

There definitely is in our society too much pressure for grievers to suppress their feelings, show no public evidence of them and bear their losses stoically. There may also be in our society too much pressure for grievers to resume their ordinary daily activities—to pick up where they were before the loss while still in the midst of acute grief.

There is nothing commendable about overprotecting grievers, but it *is* desirable to realize that they can benefit from the presence and help of sensitive, empathic people who know that grievers are affected in their grief by factors like restlessness and circular thinking and are willing to stand by and provide appropriate help. Whether that help is perhaps providing transportation, or running errands, or enabling grievers to see various alternatives as they make their decisions, it will be beneficial to them in healthfully working through the process of grief.

10

I Don't Think
I Can Make It

Feeling torn and frightened

Can it be that grief is the most painful experience of life?

Well, certainly any answer to that question will be highly subjective; but I am confident that any poll-taker could come up with a significant percentage of people who would say "yes." And they would undoubtedly all be people who had experienced deep grief first hand.

In the book, *Up from Grief,* Bernadine Kreis describes the experience this way:

Your body is weary, your emotions raw. Your heartache is a real physical ache and you are sure your life is destroyed. Your emotions are a mixture of childish anger that "this should happen to me" and a mature awareness that the one you loved is gone. You feel trapped, betrayed and frightened. You feel guilt, anger, self-pity, and you long to share all these contradictory feelings with someone who understands, but you are afraid. You wonder if you are going insane because you do not know if anyone else has ever felt as you feel.

For want of a more sophisticated term I have phrased this particular dynamic of the grief experience "torn and frightened within." They are words which I have heard grievers themselves use repeatedly to describe their feeling. I myself have experienced the loss of my father, my mother, my son and my uncle (stepfather), and this is precisely how I have felt in my grief—literally torn to pieces inside and very much afraid.

Deep depression envelops grievers and waves of tearful, agonized longing pour over them so that normal people begin to wonder if they are losing their mind. The isolation of being cut off from relationship continually rips through their insides and leaves them with the feeling of burning mental pain. The grievers wonder if they can make it through. Even though hope is inherent in mourning, they still wonder if they can make it through, and often doubt that they can. It would, in fact, be easier to lose their mind.

The memories and thoughts or mental images of the lost loved one keep coming into the griever like waves on the beach. So many things—simple, everyday things —can set off these thoughts and images because the relationship with the lost loved one involved so many aspects of the griever's life. The reminders seem to be especially painful and intense at night when the occupation and distractions of the day are not present to crowd the griever's thoughts.

And then there are the "other" images—the illusion of hearing or seeing or feeling the presence of the dead person. Some studies indicate that 50 percent of the persons grieving the loss of a spouse through death have hallucinatory experiences of the dead spouse. When this occurs to some grievers they are almost convinced they are going insane. However for many people it is peculiarly comforting and not distressing.

Sometimes grievers may misinterpret ordinary household sounds; for instance an outside noise may sound like a key turning in a door lock, or a creaking floor board may cause them to believe they heard the footstep of the deceased. Grievers may find themselves turning expectantly to an empty chair or looking expectantly into an empty room.

Grievers may get a fleeting glimpse of a face in a large crowd which quickly blends into the sea of faces, or a figure on the street which disappears into a doorway, and think that they have seen the lost loved one. Grieving people sometimes have the "feeling" of the dead person in the same room, in the bed, or in the car. Sometimes grievers awaken at night with the compelling certainty that a dead spouse is walking around downstairs, or a dead teenager is playing records or a dead child is crying in his room.

Sometimes grievers get caught up in visiting old familiar places, hoping that they might find the lost loved one there. Again grievers, in the midst of one of these illusions, may actually search for the deceased and call him or her.

On occasion the griever may experience an actual but transient hallucination of the deceased.

Whether these experiences are more disturbing or more comforting to the individual griever, it is certain that they are normal. Grieving people should be assured that this seeming abnormality *is* normal and not unusual. Such experiences occur commonly in the course of grief work and are clearly a part of the slow process of saying good-bye.

A griever tends to continue to experience the presence of the deceased because his perceptual set was tuned into the deceased before he or she died. The closer the relationship—the more "valuable" the lost loved one—the deeper the tuning in of the griever's perceptual set to the deceased. So it is reasonable that nearly everything in the griever's experience is a reminder of the deceased and there is a constant readiness to "see" and "hear" the deceased as well as a direction of attention of those parts of the griever's environment where the lost loved one was likely to be found.

We have come to view the process of grief as a slow and gradual adaptation to the sudden and absolute separation from a loved one. Such an ultimate and final total separation is frankly too much to accept or even comprehend all at once. So we hold onto memories and experiences and images of the seeming presence of the

lost loved one, and as we slowly let them go we gradually say good-bye.

The griever leaves the deceased bit by bit in a process
which is similar to that of a loved one leaving another
for a long journey. Psychiatrist Robert White, in an
article in *The American Family Physician,* described
it this way:

> The traveler embraces and stands looking and
> longing and embraces again until the final parting.
> He walks away, looks back, embracing from a dis-
> tance with eyes and words of farewell. Then at the
> door of the train or plane, he pauses again and
> turns to wave yet another good-bye. And then, as
> the train or plane begins to move, he looks and
> waves from the window until, out of sight, he is
> left only with memories. But in idle moments, and
> especially at night, the traveler is reunited with his
> loved one in his imagination.

This imagery is, I believe, very appropriate to the
grief experience; for this is the way it seems to be with
the *final* journey—the parting through death. We can
probably only bear the pain of parting through this
slow and gradual process of saying good-bye to our
memories of the lost loved one. And even though the
agony of it may be the most painful experience of life,
if grievers avoid it, the good-bye is never completed.
And until it is, grievers remain impaired in their abili-
ty and capacity to return their attention fully to the
world of the living.

11

Holding Together

I'm going to make it!

The experience of a loss is an uncharted territory; grievers are in a land they have never been in before. Certainly it is true that a griever may learn from experiences of loss and have some general idea of the terrain as a result of them; but still, each loss is unique unto itself, and the journey through it can be charted only as grievers make their way.

It is a scary thing; grievers fear that they may get lost in this journey and perish either on the barren sands or in the impenetrable jungle or in the pitch-darkness of night, however one envisions it. And some do. Some people break down, some people are emotionally damaged for life, some people even commit suicide. For some the agony of grief is so unbearable that death becomes more desirable than life.

Still in all, it seems that one of the greatest challenges for us human beings in our experience of life is to wrestle with the powers of darkness and to steal from them the glow of light; to struggle with the demons and to extract from them a divine blessing; to wrench out of a black and evil experience, something positive and growth-producing.

Every experience of loss provides the griever with the possibility of personal-emotional-spiritual growth. Hope *is* inherent in grief. It is of utmost importance for grievers not to lose sight of this. Not that they constantly dwell upon that throughout the grief process— that is impossible to do with authenticity. Indeed it is sometimes virtually obliterated by the monstrous depression and despair, and the searing anger and guilt of grief. But rather that it is *never* completely crushed, but rises up again and again, ultimately to bloom.

Growing up in our experience of life seems to be a process that ends only when life itself ends. Growing up is simply laying aside bit by bit the childish notion that I am the center of the universe and the childish expectation that all of creation must orbit around me. Certainly I may know *intellectually* that I cannot everlastingly have my way, but true maturity comes only as I *experientially* surrender—or if you will, *die* —atom by atom to this innate egocentricity. Crying is indeed an excellent vehicle for the discharge of my feelings of grief over my loss; but crying will not bring back the dead.

Human growth involves the laying aside or surrendering of those cherished, albeit grandiose, childish expectations, while still retaining an appropriate self-esteem and positive self-image. It necessitates facing reality honestly. No human being can grow personally-emotionally-spiritually by wearing rose-colored glasses or by pulling the wool over his eyes. Because in my experience I have seen in people such a tendency to do this, I am compelled to put it down as strongly as I can.

There is nothing to be gained, but only harm to be done by cherishing a Pollyanna attitude. There is certainly the potential for positive growth in the experience of deep loss. But grievers can possess that growth only after they have successfully fought and conquered the dragons that guard the gate to it. And those dragons are all the dynamics of grief that I have mentioned in the preceding pages, and more—guilt, anger, wailing, despair, depression, denial, fear, anxiety, etc. You simply do not reach the "promised land" without first wandering woefully through the wilderness.

But let it not be understood that the listing in this book of the elements common to the grief process is meant to be complete and exhaustive. Nor is it to be understood that the table of contents necessarily forms their chronological "order of appearance." In fact, not all these elements need necessarily be present in every experience of grief, not even by the same person. Nor need they necessarily be present to the same degree in every person. What *is* to be understood is that there *are* dynamic feelings present in the person experiencing grief; and allowing the agonizing experience of going to pieces in the process of grief to happen is precisely what will hold the griever together in an integrated and healthy whole and truly make him or her a more complete and fulfilled human being because of it. The research done on grieving persons is consistently conclusive: Persons who are open to and allow expression of their manifold feelings of the experience of grief— who manifest severe bouts of sobbing, agitation, depression, longing, guilt, anger, rationalization, etc.—are least distressed and incapacitated when interviewed at periodic intervals following the trauma of a loss. They tend also to be more re-integrated and emotionally-spiritually stable. On the other hand, persons who manifested little or no expression of the feelings incorporated in the grief experience were the most disturbed and incapacitated when interviewed.

Avoiding or encouraging the avoidance of the expression of emotion which is necessary for effective grief work seems then, to work to the detriment of the griever. "You'll be alright," "Time will heal," "God will take care of you," and other similar simplistic euphemisms may sound uplifting, supportive and even righteous; but they are little more than palliatives which deny the depth and the severity of the griever's wound and promise cheap healing which simply cannot happen.

Grief work is just that—work. It is the sweat and tears and agony of adapting in a legion of ways to the loss, and endeavoring to fill the void created by it. It is using energy to review in detail the aspects of life which were meaningful and enriched by association with the lost one. It is realizing in each of these aspects of life that the loss is painful and the loss is permanent. It is resigning oneself to the inevitable—and *that* is to suffer pain. And grievers are able to get through each of these aspects only when they have managed to achieve independence from the lost one in each of the individual aspects.

Sooner or later the question of time enters into the experience of grief, and grievers say, "How long will it take?" "Will I never get over this?" "Is this never going to end?" "When is it going to end?" There are certainly a great many answers for these questions available from lay people and professionals alike; but there are so many variables involved in the experience of grief that I believe it is risky business to make any kind of generalization at all concerning time in the grief experience. About the only thing one can say with any certitude is, "It depends."

The variables include such factors as the basic personality of the griever; how "experienced" the griever is in dealing with loss; how the griever has dealt with other losses—i.e. pattern of coping with trauma; the relationship of this loss to other losses; the nature of this loss; the worth or "value" of the lost loved object to the griever and how much he or she cared about the lost loved object; etc.

Actually the duration of grief depends largely upon the success of the grievers in doing their grief work:

in becoming free from the bondage to the deceased, in readjusting to the environment wherein the deceased is missing, and filling the void left by the deceased.

The duration of grief varies from person to person and even from experience to experience within the same person. It also varies from researcher to researcher and author to author. There seems to be some division of agreement concerning time, although the period of one year for the process of grief seems to appear frequently in the literature. Still, one researcher who studied 72 widows found that after *two* years following their loss only *ten* were free from grief.

My suspicion is that our greatest error lies in being in too great a hurry for feelings to disappear and for grief work to be completed. Certainly the intensity of the experience of grief diminishes with time, but its presence continues on within the griever for a longer period than many of us care to believe. We seem to have a tendency to hurry grievers along. In "nice" ways we say, "Don't you think it's about time you snapped out of it?" Grievers sometimes say that to themselves, wanting to meet the expectations of society: "Let's see now, it's been a year. I *should* be snapping out of it."

My own understanding of the duration of grief was broadened by a personal experience. The loss of our baby son just three days after his birth was a terrible experience for Marilyn and me. We thought for a time that we wouldn't be able to get over it; the pain was so agonizing. Months passed and we slowly and wearily made our adjustments. Then a year—and more.

One day about a year and a half after his death we received word that the child of friends of ours had died. The little boy had been a beautiful child but suffered from leukemia. We all knew that his days were limited, but now the last one had come. There was no public funeral service in the mortuary for the boy, rather a memorial service in the church where he and his family had attended.

I remember that the day was a rather bleak day. There was a light, but cold rain falling as Marilyn and I got out of our car and walked into the church. We were a bit early, but we took a seat in the quiet church and waited for the service to begin. I do not recall where my thoughts went as I sat there in the quiet, but I still remember with stark clarity how I was suddenly thrust back into my own grief of a year and a half previous. As a prelude to the memorial service the organist began playing softly the music of *Jesus Loves Me, This I Know*. And before she had completed half a stanza the notes had torn open my old wound; the words, "Little ones to him belong" pulled at the wound; and I wept and wept right there in the pew, and Marilyn right along with me.

The only thing I remember from the memorial service is how hot and burning tears can be.

After the service had ended Marilyn and I managed to make it back to our automobile. And there we cried still more, and wondered aloud, "God, will we never get over this?"

It had been a year and a half since the death of our baby; and I would have bet a month's salary that we were more or less successfully through the process of grieving his loss. But I was wrong. And I learned very painfully that I needed much more time to "get over" my loss than I ever thought I would.

My experience is also a good illustration of how important and necessary it is to realize that there may be what appear to be periods of real *regression* in the process of grief work, and that this too, is a normal experience. The line of recovery from the pits of agonized depression back up to the normalcy of adjustment to the loss is not a straight one, ever onward and ever upward. It looks more like the daily charting of the Dow Jones Industrial Average. It is not at all unusual for a real gain in working through the feelings of the loss experience to be achieved, only to be wiped out by the return of an acute attack of grief which was triggered by an occurrence or experience somehow related to the original loss.

The stimuli capable of triggering the return of acute grief are also variable and unique to the individual griever. Some of the more common are holidays, anniversaries, birthdays, geographic places, songs, books, another death, etc. In my experience, the death of our friends' son did not reactivate my grief. Nor did going into the church and sitting down waiting for the memorial service to begin. It was the music of the song, and the words which it evoked in my memory that triggered the acute attack of grief.

A widower whose wife had been dead for two and a half years was flying from Minneapolis to Boston. It was a clear, bright day, and the view of the ground was superb. But superb or not he had some papers to look over in preparation for his business in Boston, so he devoted his attention to them rather than to the view from the window. After a while, when he had finished his reading he leaned down to get his brief-case and his glance happened to go out the window to the ground below. And his heart almost stopped. There, just ahead, bathed in brilliant sunshine and haloed with their own mist, lay the majestic Niagara Falls . . . the site of his honeymoon, twenty-seven years before.

He could not stop the tears. Nor did he try.

It is a healthy and helpful thing to be able to express feelings; it is indeed one of the crowning glories of our humanity. In all our experiences of life we may find deeper fulfillment by being aware of and acting appropriately on our feelings. But particularly in the experience of grief do we benefit from this innate therapeutic blessing.

Grief is good medicine for the sickness of loss. It restores wholeness. And the truth of the paradox abides: as you go to pieces grieving, you *are* held to-gether.

Epilog

Diary of an Encounter with Grief

The following account was written by Chaplain Kenneth G. Reiners, a chaplain at Fairview Hospital, Minneapolis, Minnesota, at the time of the death of his father-in-law, Mr. William C. Falk. It is, I believe, an accurate sketch of the manifold experience of grief over loss.

Monday, January 14

9:30 A.M. I am sitting in my office writing a letter. The phone rings and shatters the silence of my room. It is my wife, Helene. She is crying. "Daddy was killed this morning!," she blurts out in her broken, sobbing voice. "Debbie?" I reply in bewilderment. And she quickly responds, "No! *Daddy,* was killed!" And my spontaneous cry is, "No, GOD, NO! . . . I'll be home right away." I hang up the receiver and I am aware that I am tapping my fingers on the desk. . . . And I cry, "God, WHY?"

10:15 A.M. I am home. The apartment door is ajar. I walk in and call, "Helene?" . . . No answer. . . . Again, "Helene?" . . . Silence. . . . I panic, and I blindly and frantically search every room crying out, "Helene?" . . . But no answer. . . . God, what an empty, lonely feeling. . . . And then Helene walks in and gently calls, "Ken?" . . . I run to her. We embrace and weep in each other's arms. And I wonder: "Is death like coming home to an empty room expecting your spouse to be there, and she's not . . . forever?"

10:45 A.M. I am at Aqualand waiting to buy a week-end feeder for Kevin's aquarium before we go home to be with Mom. I am impatient. I begin tapping my fingers on the glass counter top. And I wonder: "My God! Doesn't that store manager know my father-in-law was killed this morning?" . . . As I anxiously wait for the manager to complete his business with a customer ahead of me, I become aware how—even in death—the lives of twelve, trifle fish become significant.

11:45 A.M. We are at our ten-year-old daughter's elementary school. She is waiting at the entrance for us. . . . God, how we dread telling her the news. . . . She gets in the car. And I tell her, "Kathy, we have sad news. Granddad died this morning. He was killed in a tractor accident." Kathy explodes with tears and the first word she utters in her sobbing, heaving voice is, "WHY?" . . . And a moment later . . . "What about Sam?" (Sam is her guinea pig). . . .

We arrive at our twelve-year-old son's junior high school. He sees us and is running to the car. "What's wrong?," he asks in a puzzled voice. . . . "Kevin, we have sad news. Granddad died this morning. He was killed in a tractor accident." Tears violently erupt and as I hold his sobbing body in my arms he asks, "What happened?" . . . And a moment later, "What about my fish?" . . . And I wonder . . . "Is life and death one?" . . .

4:30 P.M. After many weary miles and a flood of tears later, we arrive at Grandma's house. She meets us at the door. We embrace and weep. I am speechless. (I once thought I knew what sorrow was. After all, hadn't I ministered daily to the dying person in the hospital? And many a time I have shared in the sorrow of strangers who lost a loved one.) But now . . . It's different. Grief is no longer a "head-trip" . . . an idea . . . but an experience. . . . And I discover it to be totally different from what I *thought* it to be. . . . And much more painful.

Tuesday, January 15

3:30 P.M. For two days now, relatives and friends have been flowing in and out of the house. They bring hot dishes, cakes, hams. They come to express their sympathy. Those who have experienced sorrow themselves understand. They express their sympathy with a touch, a tear, a hug . . . while others feel awkward, embarrassed and stumble with words. . . . A few are insensitive. . . . An auctioneer neighbor is pressing Mom as to what she plans to do with the milk cows . . . he wants to sell them for her. . . . Another is boistrous and loud. He has diarrhea of the mouth . . . words without meaning. . . . How tragic that a touch, a hug, a tear . . . are pleasures and privileges our culture teaches us to keep away from.

8:00 P.M. We are in the funeral home. As we stand beside the casket and look at Granddad's face, Kathy weeps softly and says: "I love him so much. I didn't want him to die." . . . She feels what we are *thinking*. . . . Kevin is stoic as he stares in silence. Helene slips her arm around his shoulders and tenderly says, "Kevin, it's okay to cry." And immediately his tears erupt like Mt. Vesuvius. . . .

On our way back to Grandma's house, Kathy interrupts our silence and tears. She says, "I only kissed Granddad once and he was so pleased. I sure wish I would have kissed him more often." . . . Again, a little child leads us and expresses the guilt we were feeling.

Wednesday, January 16

9:00 A.M. It is two mornings past Granddad's death. Mom is at the barn cleaning and washing the milkers. Helene and her sisters insisted that they do it for her, but she wanted to do it herself. . . . Perhaps we can be too helpful in times like these. And maybe, this is Mom's way of saying, "Life must go on for me."

12:00 noon. We are gathered around the dinner table. All of Helene's brothers and sisters are present. They are reminiscing and recalling humorous stories of their childhood related to their father. "Pops" and "Daddy," they call him. We all laugh heartily. . . . Somehow, it seems to ease and soothe the sting and pain of death.

Thursday, January 17

3:00 p.m. The funeral is over. We are slowly driving to the cemetery. Kevin interrupts our solemn thoughts and silence. He asks, "Did that man really live 969 years?" (The pastor had mentioned in his funeral message something about Methuselah living that long.) I reply, "Kevin, in those days they had a different understanding of time than we do now." . . . He appears to be satisfied . . . and I wonder why he asked?

4:00 P.M. We have returned from the cemetery and are in the church social hall for lunch and to share our good-byes with friends and relatives. I greet the pastor and thank him for his ministry to the family. My voice falters and tears come to my eyes. I share with him that this is really one time when I most needed to be ministered to. And he replies, "Have faith and God will see you through." And he briskly walks away . . . leaving me standing . . . alone . . . in the center of the room and feeling like . . . I needed his ministry still. . . .

Friday, January 18

10:30 A.M. We are opening and reading the sympathy cards . . . it seems like thousands. . . . I find myself reading only those cards where there is a hand-written, personal message. . . . The others seem so scientific and businesslike.

Sunday, January 20

3:30 P.M. We are on our way home. We kiss and hug Grandma good-bye. We depart in tears feeling the absence of Granddad's wave and his cheery good-bye. Our highway passes the cemetery where he is buried. It seems so cold and lonely. . . . Helene weeps softly as we drive by. I reach out and grasp her hand. . . . There's silence. . . . Only the drone of the car motor can be heard until Kevin and Kathy interrupt our silence with, "What is heaven and hell like? Who is God and what is he like?" And we spend the remainder of our trip discussing theology.

Monday, January 21

5:00 P.M. It has been a sluggish day for me at the hospital. I find my mind pre-occupied with Granddad's death. It interferes with my daily routine. . . . Today I found myself looking in the yellow pages of the phone book for a residential number. After finally locating the number, I dialed the wrong number twice. . . . Sometimes I find myself rushing to do things. It's like I was rushing after time or trying to catch up with time. . . . Could it be that I am still caught up in the anxiety of all that has happened since Granddad's death? Or am I more aware of the value of time . . . and living?

Friday, January 25

6:00 P.M. We are on our way home to be with Grandma again. This will be her first weekend alone since the funeral. There's a beautiful sunset in the sky as we approach her home. As I gaze at the beauty and splendor of the golden haze reflected on the clouds, I think of Granddad. . . . And somehow, heaven seems a little more real to me.

Friday, February 1

7:00 p.m. It has been almost three weeks now, since "Daddy" died. Tonight, is the first night I am aware that Helene is feeling stronger and in better spirits. I too, feel more together again. It seems as though it took ages of rest and sleep. The emotional and physical drain of grief has been overwhelming. There remains an ache in our hearts. We are aware that a part of our lives is missing. And we wonder . . . will the ache *ever* leave us? Probably never completely . . . but healing *does* take place, and we are beginning to feel it.